Jeroninio "Jerry" Almeida
Jyoti Nanda

Karma Kurry

for the mind, body, heart & soul

COLLECTOR'S EDITION

GU00504252

JAICO PUBLISHING HOUSE

Ahmedabad Bangalore Bhopal Bhubaneswar Chennai
Delhi Hyderabad Kolkata Lucknow Mumbai

Published by Jaico Publishing House
A-2 Jash Chambers, 7-A Sir Phirozshah Mehta Road
Fort, Mumbai - 400 001
jaicopub@jaicobooks.com
www.jaicobooks.com

© Jeroninio Almeida & Jyoti Nanda

KARMA KURRY
ISBN 978-81-8495-403-6

First Jaico Impression: 2015

No part of this book may be reproduced or utilized in
any form or by any means, electronic or
mechanical including photocopying, recording or by any
information storage and retrieval system,
without permission in writing from the publishers.

Printed by
Pashupati Printers
1/429/16, Gali No. 1, Friends Colony
Industrial Area, G. T. Road, Shahdara, Delhi - 95

To the memory of my closest friend SavioDesa who became one with God on September 18, 2013.

Table of Contents

Preface

Madiba (Nelson Mandela)

When I first conceptualized the *Karma Kurry* series of books, I wished that someone humble and modest would write a foreword for my book. However, I felt that the only living legend, who could do justice to this book is Madiba (Nelson Mandela), who dedicated his life to the cause of social justice, fairness and equality for one and all. Thus, I wrote to him in early 2012, and he promised to write a foreword for *Karma Kurry for the Mind, Body, Heart and Soul*. Today, Mandela, who is 94 years old, remains hospitalized and is listed in critical condition after being diagnosed with a lingering lung infection and I felt it would be inappropriate to trouble him at this time. At the same time, I wish for no one else to write a foreword as only Madiba could have done justice to this book. Hence, I share below what Madiba wrote to us when we requested him for a foreword.

Dear Jeroninio,

"These stories are awe-inspiring and compellingly powerful. Usually most books have one story, one chapter, one idea or one hero that inspires you and has the power to change a person's life. Going by what I have read, all of *Karma Kurry for the Mind, Body, Heart and Soul* stories have that power to inspire people to rise and act to make a difference. The five stories, which I have read are all so life changing and shall surely inspire everyone who reads

Karma Kurry for the Mind, Body, Heart and Soul to try and make a difference in our world. **I am sure that this unique book of extraordinary, everyday unsung and unassuming heroes from the world over shall inspire many more ordinary people like you, me and everyone to become extraordinary heroes."** – Nelson Mandela

Introduction

Namaste to all of you and thank you for choosing to read *Karma Kurry for the Mind, Body, Heart and Soul.*

In 2003, two movements – the Karma Mitra and The Joy of Giving (JOG) – were launched with the idea of changing the mindset and attitude of people in such a way that they decided to be the change by fulfilling their own Individual Social Responsibility (ISR). Since then, JOG has become a huge movement in India, has raised funds for several causes and is being emulated in several other countries.

Around the same time that we were promoting JOG a decade ago, I was asked to host a program with HRH Prince Charles, the Prince of Wales who was visiting India. I decided to hold not a fundraiser, but a simple and austere ceremony, where the prince would recognize invisible heroes from our society. Prince Charles then honored and celebrated four unsung citizen-heroes of the society for their extraordinary work: Ms Mogalamma, a 22-year-old slum dweller working for the polio-affected; Mr Saddam Basha, an auto rickshaw driver promoting peace and communal harmony; Mr Mahadev Rajmane, a prisoner working for legal rights; and Ms Mangala Khillo, a bonded laborer who did marvelous work for labor rights.

Thus, were born the egalitarian KARMAVEER PURASKAAR and the 'RIGHT every WRONG movement' under the aegis of iCONGO (a confederation of NGOs) and Karma Mitra Foundation. The core objective of these movements was promoting INDIVIDUAL SOCIAL RESPONSIBILTY, wherein each one of us becomes and leads the change we want to see in our society.

I remember in 2004, my planning the awards raised a few eyebrows; especially when I declared my intent to create an austere awards ceremony and a democratic platform that would be shared with equal respect and dignity by royal dignitaries, captains of industry, celebrities, sex-workers, slum dwellers, street-children, youth and people from all walks of life. Today, we can proudly declare that we have created that **egalitarian platform** through the **Karmaveer Puraskaar** (Awards) for Citizen Social Justice and Action, where people from diverse fields come together to make a huge difference with their simple but significant citizen actions.

My decade-long experience has further entrenched this belief. It fired me with an enthusiasm for sharing these inspiring stories of our Karmaveer heroes and thus was born the idea for *Karma Kurry*, a book that would democratize heroism by telling stories of ordinary people doing their extraordinary citizen actions.

The desired outcome of this book is to inspire more and more people to become everyday heroes who can make a difference in our world. While on one hand, we stand up and speak out to fight social injustice and wrongdoings, on the other hand, it is important to create heroes who start making a difference with their simple actions and great love for humanity in their hearts. This kind of love can change everything.

Storytelling is the most powerful way to put ideas into the world today.

– Robert McKee

Every human being has a hero within, and if we unleash this hero within every person by inspiring him/her to make a difference in our world, then a better world is possible. Yes, we can find positive solutions to all social issues when each of us awakens that hero within to do something small, simple and yet significant enough to make that difference. I have been sharing these inspiring stories of our Karmaveer heroes in conferences I speak at and training programs I conduct. However, I felt that a better way to connect would be to tell the stories through a series of books. This gave birth to the idea of *Karma Kurry for the Mind, Body, Heart and Soul*. I thought of this title as Karma and Kurry, both are eastern concepts and humanity has benefited in a huge way with Eastern Wisdom that gave the world so many concepts like the zero, the first urban civilization and economic system, the science of public administration and preventive and curative medicine, among others. Being a huge learner of Eastern Wisdom and the best practices of the West, I felt that together the two words (Karma and Kurry) would describe perfectly the concept behind the series – a wonderful mix of heartwarming stories from all over the globe, stirred and cooked together to inspire and motivate people to recognize their **own power of one and thus help others be the change and lead the change by practicing Individual Social Responsibility.**

> *Stories are how we learn. The progenitors of the world's religions understood this, handing down our great myths and legends from generation to generation.*
> – Bill Mooney and David Holt,
> The Storyteller's Guide

Stories that speak of the power of human potential appeal not only to children but also to adults. For children, they are magical journeys into a wonderful world, while these stories help adults model their lives, mindsets, attitudes and behaviors. It has been scientifically proven that human beings idolize their chosen heroes and start behaving like them. Hence, it is even more important to tell our children and youth the great stories of real heroes who have emerged to become extraordinary people in an ordinary world by practicing human values and fulfilling their Individual Social Responsibility. *Karma Kurry* would, therefore, have strong philosophical leanings and will narrate stories of people who have done things with their heart, mind, body and soul; for the betterment of humanity. Most people you will meet in this book, will excite you and their stories will inspire you at a profound level. These people are champions of change, heroic women and men who turned their defeats, infirmities and adversities into laudable actions for change. They changed their own lives for the better and also the lives of several others. They converted their ordinary human existence into greatness by being the change. The message they bring to you is that none of us need to be an ordinary person as each and every one of us possesses extraordinary greatness, capabilities and immense potential to be the change and make a difference. And it all begins with discovering the purpose of our life and what is it that we can do to create a better world for future generations between our life and death. That is what separates the ordinary from the great.

It takes a thousand voices to tell a single story.
– a Native American proverb

This book has taken almost two years to compile. It has hundreds of thousands of voices and some of the best story-tellers narrating you stories of the Karmaveer heroes.

Yes, that's the model we follow, where the stories are being told by eminent and prolific writers (including Gregory David Roberts of *Shantaram fame;* Anita Pratap a globally renowned journalist and others) of our times to create a great and a first-of-its-kind reading experience. We promise you that the stories in *Karma Kurry* will inspire great ideas in your mind, elicit encouraging feelings in your heart and incite the great human spirit within you to live more, love more, become more and do more to be the change and say I *CAN* DO something to bring about a change in our society, nation and world. The author-proceeds from the sale of *Karma Kurry* will be used to recognize and support real heroes and the causes they espouse.

Everyone is necessarily the hero of his own life story.
— John Barth

You may also have your story or the story of someone you know that is inspiring and needs to be told to inspire others to help them awaken the hero within. You may also have a great human interest story or an inspiring anecdote that you wish to tell. If so, please do write to me and I shall respond to each and all of you within a week of receiving your mail. To interact with me, you may write to me at jerrylearns2learn121@gmail.com or follow me on social media through www.jerrylearns2learn.com.

Thank you for all your support and solidarity.

Jai Hind and warm regards,

Jeroninio Almeida

Treading the Unbeaten Path

Anita Pratap

"Growing up, I wanted to be a doctor," says Anita Pratap, one of India's finest journalists. "But, I scored less in my biology examination in class XI, so, pursuing medicine was not an option," she adds. She admits that she felt dejected, and was forced to consider an alternative course. Her teachers encouraged her to take up literature, a subject she had excelled in. It took a bit of nudging, for Anita didn't see it as something that would equip her with a functional skill. "I am a very practical person," she says. However, enroll she did for a bachelor's in English literature at New Delhi's famous Miranda House, hardly realizing that she had taken the first step towards a promising future.

Determined to be a working woman, Anita knew that whatever she studied had to allow her a career. Following her bachelor's degree (where she was a class-topper), she completed a one-year post-graduate diploma course in journalism at Bangalore University. Anita says that her college years left her with a sense of futility and offered her no solid skills that she could use at work. However, this changed with an internship, during her course, at the *Indian Express* whose editor at that time was reputed journalist Arun Shourie. Her two months there were catalytic, and they opened the doors to the world she was born to inhabit.

"My first story during the internship was on lion-tailed macaques and their dwindling numbers," Anita

1

remembers. Soon, more stories, even mainstream ones, came her way and Anita realized that she loved reporting. She liked meeting people, and it seemed that her destiny had found her.

A year later, on completion of her course, she was back at the *Indian Express;* this time as a staff reporter, based in Bengaluru. She entered the office eager to begin her days in pursuit of political and investigative stories. But, to her dismay, her first assignment was to cover the inauguration of a toy train at the city park! Her colleague, looking at her disappointment, told her, "This is where you start." "The scales fell from my eyes that day," she says. Undeterred, she did the stories that were assigned to her. But, she refused to lose sight of where she wanted to be. "I took my ideas to the chief reporter and he said I should do what I was assigned," she says. Anita began to use her spare time to pursue her ideas, writing stories that even the chief reporter could not ignore for too long. He started publishing them and within a year, Anita says, she was doing exactly what she wanted.

A break came in 1980, when the *Sunday Magazine* offered her a job in Chennai. Now defunct, it was then India's bestselling English news magazine that focused on politics. Anita joined it as a correspondent. She studied the socio-politico changes emerging from the severe rift between the Sri Lankan Tamils and the Sinhalese. She followed the story with great interest, her curiosity leading her towards it. Little news trickled in, but when she read about the Jaffna Public Library being burned down by "miscreants," she knew that something was afoot. "I started digging deeper and knew that we were standing before a looming crisis," she says. In 1983, riots broke out in Sri Lanka and even as the world wondered what was going on, Anita set out to coax her editor and asked for the assignment. Expectedly, he was reluctant to send her as it was dangerous and she was so young, and a woman!

"I fought for that story. I had done the research and had the right contacts. Not being sent to cover a story in a danger zone, on account of me being a woman, was a completely unacceptable excuse," she says. Anita was then 24 years of age and had a young son, but nothing could stop her. She didn't want anything to. Her editor relented and she was on her way to foreign shores.

It was the worst time to be in Sri Lanka. The mood was anti-Indian and anti-Tamil. Anita moved around the city with her camera, as anonymously as possible, blending in with the locals and capturing the terror of the riots. Once caught by the police for photographing a burning building, she pretended to be an architecture student on research work. Being a woman became an advantage, for no one assumed that a woman journalist would be sent to cover a dangerous conflict zone. She returned to Chennai five days later and wrote her story supported by pictures, which became the first such detailed report on the issue. The report made it to the Indian parliamentary session. Anita had arrived as a journalist.

Although she was being congratulated for her reporting, and lauded for being brave, Anita remembers how deeply affected she was. "For three days after I returned, my hands trembled as the horror of what I had seen hit me," she adds. Professionally, she had crossed a milestone.

In 1985, Anita separated from her husband. With her young son, she moved to Bengaluru to work at the *India Today* magazine. Some months later, she got a call offering her a job at *TIME* magazine, based in New Delhi.

Anita began moving up the reporting ladder. Throughout her career, Anita was presented with a ringside view of history. And what she saw wasn't just news being made and history being written. She saw past the smoke and dust, into the lives of individuals. She saw the impact of war on children and how the future was going to be shaped from such a present. She began to show the human side of war, conflict and violence. Wherever she went, Kashmir or Afghanistan or Sri Lanka, Anita sought stories that revealed what she calls "the real tragedy of war".

Anita was a part of a generation of reporters, who highlighted problems that needed a solution. They called themselves the typewriter guerrillas, exposing corruption and power politics. "In my time, we were seen as the solution. Judges and journalists were the last resort. Journalism was a tool to make India better. Today, it's a blunt weapon and a toothless tool. As a journalist, what motivated me was to be the voice of the nameless and faceless people, who have no power and no money. I have always been on the side of the underdog. But, today's journalists seem to have surrendered this role to the corporate machinery. The democracy has been hijacked by corporate lobbies and the journalists have become a part of the problem," she says. For eight years, she continued with *TIME*, growing too comfortable for her own liking. There were few options, so she continued working there until an evening when, at a private dinner hosted for Ed Turner, one of CNN's head honchos, she found herself seated at the head table.

"At the table were Ed Turner, HK Dua, the head of The *Times of India* and Najma Heptullah, a member of parliament. During dinner, Ed leaned towards me and told me to join CNN. I remember HK Dua saying, 'You want to take away our best journalist!' Najma Heptullah too interjected saying, 'We cannot lose Anita to CNN'. Perhaps, this made Ed more determined to hire me. We agreed to meet the next day and he made me an offer I could not refuse," she recollects.

For someone who likes to constantly reinvent herself, working for CNN came at an opportune moment. It offered her the challenge of television and she learned everything all over again, translating what she knew of the print medium to fit the visual medium. There was much to keep her hooked. Now, her reporting reached the whole world almost immediately with the feedback being instantaneous. The downside was that she had no more than two minutes per story and felt the frustration of touching the surface without digging deeper. There was no time or space for perspectives to emerge. Once again, she chose to fight for what she believed were important stories – those that lay below the surface.

For instance, in Bangladesh, she found that over a period of 20 years, the birth rate had reduced by half. When she pitched this fact as a story, her editors in the US dismissed it. Shortly afterwards Anita went to Bangladesh to cover the political change, and she chose to stay back to follow up on her idea. It led to a 23-minute documentary that turned out to be so popular that CNN aired it repeatedly. Anita had again shut her detractors and naysayers.

A television journalist now, she missed the anonymity of the print medium. But, times were changing and television was growing in popularity. People, it seemed were reading less, and so she continued at CNN, also making documentaries in her spare time. And she always told the story of the common man whose cause she championed.

Amid her hectic schedules, Anita fondly recalls the pleasant breaks her son used to give her. "My son thought that I had a cushy job. For a long time, he thought it was the best job in the world. I rubbed shoulders with celebrities, intellectuals and people in power and that was the only side he had seen. One day, I decided it was time to show him the reality of my job. I had to cover a story in Varanasi and took him along. He was only around 10 years of age then. We flew to Varanasi and checked into a five-star hotel. So far the trip was living up to his expectations. But, I had to leave immediately to cover the story and took him along. The whole day was spent in reporting my story and it was past midnight when we returned to the hotel. There was no time for dinner and by dawn we were on our way back to New Delhi. We missed many meals that day, but my son no longer assumed I was leading a charmed life," she says.

For 14 years, she was a single, working mother, balancing home and career with ease. With her son in college and her CNN days behind her, Anita slipped into yet another new role – that of a diplomat's wife. In 1999, she married Arne Walther, then Norwegian ambassador to India.

It was around then that she chose to take time off to write her memoir. "I had not spoken about the things I had seen or heard with anyone. And sitting in Norway dredging out those memories, thorns embedded in my psyche, which I had to pull out one by one, was my catharsis. It took me two years to write the book and it was only during the writing of it did I allow myself to break down in remembrance of the horrors of the past," she says. Titled *Island of Blood,* this book created publishing history when the first edition sold out within a week. Two more sell-out editions followed, but for Anita that meant that she could finally move on to authoring books.

Her next book, *Unsung*, came out in 2007. A photo book co-authored with photographer Mahesh Bhat, it chronicles the lives of nine ordinary Indians who have achieved something extraordinary for their communities. Again, it was the appeal of the underdog that took Anita into the recesses of the country to reveal some fascinating accounts of the real heroes.

Despite being away from the media in the last few years, Anita continues to view life as a reporter. Being a journalist has for long defined who she has been and it's not a mantle she can shake off easily. Being a diplomat's wife has drawn her into the world that she once viewed from the outside. "It has been an eye-opener to see how power works from within. It is a learning experience. I get to meet the greatest minds and the most interesting people without the pressure of deadlines. I have been learning about other countries, studying their growth trajectories, and seeing how countries have managed their progress. I have no clue what the future will bring but that's how it has always been. I only know that I am preparing for it, for whatever the next stage is. The unknown is less frightening today," she says.

Anita now lives in Japan with her husband. Her itinerary includes official events, fundraisers, talks, speeches and the occasional commentary that she agrees to write. But perhaps, it's only a matter of time before the curtain will rise once again on the yet unknown but nevertheless promising next act.

Biographer

Aravinda Anantharaman is a Bangalore-based writer. She has authored three books for children, *Dorje's Holiday at the Gyenso Khang, Dolma Visits the City* and *Puffin Lives: The 14th Dalai Lama.*

Heroism is discovering our purpose in life, exercising the power of one and affirming the power of intent, with which we are all blessed. This seriousness of intent and honesty of purpose can help individuals awaken the hero within themselves.

– Jeroninio

In the Spirit of Arghyam (A Humble Offering)

Rohini Nilekani

Visitors who don't know either Arghyam or its founder might well imagine that Rohini Nilekani has located the foundation's office in a bungalow that carries her name. But nothing could be further from the truth. It is a quirk of chance, and a bit of an in-joke, that the foundation she set up has its office in a rented house called 'Rohini'.

Seeing the signboard of Arghyam, in a quiet middle-class neighborhood of Bengaluru, someone might at first glance mistake it for a religious organization. 'Arghyam' evokes images of sacred offerings. 'Argha' is the Sanskrit word for an offering to *devas*. Most traditional *pujas* begin with ritual-offerings of milk, curd, blades of grass and grains of rice – each of these symbolizing plentitude and well-being.

A closer look at the Arghyam signboard reveals the motto: 'safe, sustainable water for all'. The organization busily working inside is entirely this – worldly. Funded by a corpus of ₹ 150 crores donated by Rohini, this foundation is one of India's leading endeavors in 'strategic philanthropy'.

What inspired Rohini to venture down this path? How is strategic philanthropy different from charity and what can it hope to achieve?

Rohini's individual journey has been shaped both by unique circumstances and traits that are innate to her personality. She has been inspired by many people – family members as well as philosophers and intellectuals she read in her youth.

9

Years ago, Rohini Soman met Nandan Nilekani at a quizzing event at Elphinstone College, Mumbai, where his IIT team had been invited. At that point, they were both living a familiar pattern shared by their peers. Both were second-born children of middle class parents who inculcated a respect for education and the simple joys of life – good books, music and travel. While Nandan was preparing to graduate from IIT with a degree in electrical engineering, Rohini was studying for her BA in French literature. After Rohini took up a job as a reporter at the *Bombay Magazine*, a publication of the *India Today* Group.

When Rohini and Nandan married in 1981, neither of them knew that it would become a milestone-year in their lives. It was in the same year that Nandan joined a small group of fellow engineers to form a company called Infosys. It is now a part of modern Indian folklore that the initial seed capital for Infosys came from the wives of the promoters. In an act of faith, backed by a willingness to take a risk, Rohini put ₹ 10,000 of her personal savings into the fledgling company, which was all she had at the time.

In those early days, the founders of Infosys were themselves going for short spells to the USA to run projects. Accompanying Nandan on these assignments, Rohini found herself living in various towns and cities of the USA – Tampa, Kenosha, Grand Rapids and Chicago – with access to excellent public libraries.

"I never forget to acknowledge exactly how much I learned from using the amazing public libraries in America," Rohini now recalls. "I disciplined myself to start from scratch and filled in the gaps in my education – reading basic physics, economics, political science, feminist literature, literary criticism and much more only through books found in the libraries that were always within walking distance from where we lived. What a debt I owe to that system for what I experienced in those seven years, when I traveled light with only four suitcases of material possessions," she adds.

On returning to a settled life in Bengaluru, Rohini plunged into a full-time job as a correspondent for the *Sunday Magazine*. She had waited to return to India to have her children – Janhavi and Nihar – who soon came along. But, it was not in her nature to be content only with raising her toddlers. So, along with her work as a journalist, she co-founded a citizens' organization called Nagarik, to ensure safer roads. That came out of the grief over a tragic car accident, which killed two of her dear friends.

But, the need to be socially engaged was not driven by the response to such a personal loss. Rohini's actions were driven by a much wider concern about justice. Where does this passion come from?

First and foremost, it is a visceral revulsion to avoidable suffering and injustice. But, there are also historical familial influences. Sadashiv 'Babasaheb' Soman, Rohini's paternal grandfather answered Mahatma Gandhi's call for volunteers to work in the poorest areas of Champaran – following the Satyagraha Movement by peasants, who had been forced to grow indigo in almost slave-like conditions. Babasaheb was among the founders of the Bhitiharwa Ashram, set up in 1917 by Gandhiji. Says Rohini, "The Champaran Satyagraha struggle was a leitmotif for our generation and the fact that my grandfather played a role in it was not just inspiring – it also gave me a personal connection to struggles for justice."

As a teenager, Rohini felt deeply moved by memories of her grandfather when he was a young man in Champaran. She longed to visit the Bhitiharwa Ashram, which she finally did in 2007, 90 years after her grandfather had founded it. "It was like a real end to an imagined journey. My grandfather's life is very inspirational because he consistently made his decisions in a larger framework outside of his narrow self-interest... And sometimes even his family's economic interest. He gave up his law practice to join the Indian National Congress," she says. However, the most crucial element of Babasaheb's legacy was not self-sacrifice but 'an extent of vision'.

In the late 1940s, Babasaheb was faced with an acute dilemma when his eldest son Bhaskar expressed a desire to enroll in the then Imperial British Navy. A man of rigid ideas or one-dimensional convictions might have disowned his son and accused him of betraying the nationalist cause. Instead, Babasaheb responded positively to Bhaskar's line of reasoning – that since freedom was now inevitable and independent India would need a strong navy, it was important to be a part of that future.

'   "My grandfather could have forbidden his son from joining the British navy, but he did not. Instead, he respected his son's vision of the future and he resigned from the Congress to facilitate my uncle's joining the navy," says Rohini. "What inspires me most is that this was not an ideological sacrifice. It taught me the importance of not locking yourself into one position or slot and instead being able to see diverse views and perspectives," she adds. Bhaskar Soman went on to serve as chief of naval staff after independence.

Her maternal family, which comprised the agriculturists in Dahanu district, north of Mumbai, Rohini observed, had long-standing traditions of philanthropic contributions to educational institutions. "As a young person with left wing ideas, I could also appreciate the struggles of the Warli tribals around Dahanu and notice both the injustice and reciprocities in their equations with the landlords. I felt it was vital to be dispassionately honest in understanding the patterns of power and injustice and how these affect everyone. But, I also refused, then, as now, to be bracketed as an 'oppressor' because of my ancestral lineage or the opportunities that came my way," remarks Rohini.

These questions and related dilemmas took on gigantic proportions when the global success of Infosys turned all the founders' families into multi-millionaires. First of all, there was joy in being part of an endeavor that was a landmark in the history of Indian business – a few professionals from typical middle-class backgrounds proving that ethical practices can be at the core of a money-making success.

This joy was tempered by a deep conviction that wealth is never truly private. Since wealth is always generated in a wider social context, no single individual or group can take full credit. Rohini passionately believes that those who happen to become rich must hold those resources in trust. This does not mean that those who have the money should not enjoy the comforts it can buy. Trusteeship need not mean living like an ascetic. Natural simplicity, says Rohini, is that which brings joy to oneself and to others – not something that is forced or done just to look right.

A faith in trusteeship also drives Rohini's engagement with various social issues. This work is not limited to philanthropic donations, but includes participation in contemporary intellectual debates – particularly in forums that influence public policy.

To begin with, both Nandan and Rohini had contributed funds to a wide variety of institutions as and when the possibilities came up – a new theatre in Dharwad, a yoga center in Bengaluru, a new hostel building at IIT Mumbai, grants to hospitals for children who could not afford certain treatments and so on. But, it was clear from the outset that this was not enough.

"I knew all along that I needed to learn how to give money away more systematically, but it took a lot of learning to figure it out," says Rohini. The American Depository Receipt of Infosys became an inflection point in this journey. This was the first time that Rohini sold shares for a substantial return and she felt it was imperative to put the entire amount in a philanthropic foundation. So Arghyam, which had already been registered in 2001, was infused with a further corpus of ₹ 100 crores, to which another ₹ 50 crores were added later. "Some friends said it was risky and unnecessary to put the entire money into this foundation, but I felt quite certain about doing this," says Rohini.

The focus on water came out of a eureka moment in April 2005. "I can hardly claim that it was a very strategic decision to work in the water space. Yes, we were researching other issues like maternal health, but one day, while having a shower I had an epiphany! As it happens, it was one of the best areas to focus on, as there was no Indian foundation then, exclusively devoted to water," she says.

Meanwhile, a great amount of learning on strategic philanthropy and volunteerism was also happening through her role as the chairperson of the Akshara Foundation, which had been set up in collaboration with the Government of Karnataka with a mission to ensure 'Every Child in School and Learning Well'. Akshara aimed to do this through a wide range of activities designed to activate communities to ensure that government schools function well and there is improvement in the lives of children.

As a co-founder and chairperson of Pratham Books, which was set up in 2004, Rohini was part of a team that turned an ambitious dream into reality – making available high quality books at very low costs to children who otherwise do not have access to such literature. At Pratham Books, says Rohini, "We have tried to create a hybrid model that spans volunteerism, markets, philanthropy and also working with the state. We have created a societal mission to give 'A book in every child's hands'."

Apart from the ten million books and an equal number of story cards that Pratham Books has put into circulation, its presence has had an impact on the sector as manifested by opening up new spaces for other publishers and reduction in prices on the whole. Pratham Books is probably also a global leader in putting the most books in the Creative Commons – where people are free to replicate the text and pictures. Rohini, who has also been one of the principal funders, is delighted at their success in 'democratizing the joy of reading'.

At Arghyam, the story has been more complex, as the organization has worked in various dimensions. As a donor, Arghyam has supported more than 90 projects across 22 states in India to improve the availability of domestic water. These projects include community management of ground-water, sustainable alternatives to salinity and fluoride as well as ecological sanitation. Instead of itself running these programs, Arghyam has been supporting NGOs working in the rural areas; many of them already having extensive ex-perience in the field of water. Arghyam has also supported several networks that aim to build the collective voice of NGO groups at the national or state level, such as the Water Conflicts Forum, the Ecological Sanitation Consortium and the Solution Exchange, which is an e-mail discussion group of water sector professionals.

From the outset, Arghyam has also undertaken some initiatives on its own. The most pathbreaking of these is the India Water Portal, an open, web-based platform for sharing knowledge, information and data amongst water sector practitioners. Another initiative ASHWAS, an activity-based citizen survey of the domestic water situation across

Karnataka covering 17,000 households. The third is the Integrated Urban Water Management project in Mulbagal, a small town in Karnataka, where the aim is to explore a model for local government-led, people-centric, source-to-sink model for urban water management in small towns. Arghyam has also been closely engaged in the national water policy dialogue through participation in committees, giving inputs to strategies, plans and schemes of related ministries, organizing civil society consultations and sharing lessons of its work and partners' work from the ground.

This extensive experience in strategic philanthropy has only deepened and refined the questions and dilemmas that have always been associated with this role. India's multiple traditions have all emphasized that 'how' you give is as important as 'what' and 'how much' is given.

"Giving away money is hard work," says Rohini. "There is a lot involved in *what* you give and *how* you give – be it money, time or energy. There is much traditional wisdom about the requisite cautions. To whom are you giving? What do you want to achieve by giving? Can you put yourself in the shoes of the receiver?" she adds.

These questions can only be resolved through living them out – by actually doing and learning. Rohini's starting point was a firm conviction that while there is a space for charity, that is not the critical need of our times. For example, funding the digging of new wells or donating water through tankers to water-starved areas might offer temporary relief, but it is unlikely to address the larger issue of water and sanitation. Strategic philanthropy aims to address the problem at its source by seeking to intervene in ways that throw up systemic solutions. This means intervening through a diverse range of specific projects, as well as engaging with both policy-makers and private companies, who have a stake in the water sector.

When it began, Arghyam was in an exploratory mode, supporting and engaging diverse initiatives in the domestic water space across many socio-geo-climatic zones and a range of topics. "This enabled us to understand the issues facing the sector at a granular level and develop our philosophy and approaches towards sustainable, equitable water management. We've been able to use the strengths of being an independent foundation to support 'risky' innovations on emerging issues," says Rohini.

This also strengthened Arghyam's ability to foster spaces for dialogue within civil society and among citizens, experts and public policy officials. "We're now consolidating the ground lessons, building on our networks and focusing on a few key areas where we, as a small foundation, can be more effective," says Sunita Nadhmuni, who served as the CEO of Arghyam from 2005 till recently. "Measuring this effectiveness is critical, but can be tricky. Strong signaling from Rohini has steered us away from the numbers game. We felt the foundational work that we support cannot be measured solely through number of villages and number of households. Rather, it is through networks sustained, capacities built, visibility given to issues and spaces created for dissenting views," adds Sunita.

For Rohini, the most crucial learning has been the need to appreciate diversity of approaches. For instance, a particular approach or method which may be perfect in a certain part of Rajasthan may not be appropriate in Bihar. This is not just because of geographic differences but because different communities see life differently. A deeper understanding of ecological limits and social disparities has created an epic struggle to redefine what constitutes the 'good life'.

Being focused on these questions and dilemmas fosters the need for both humility and a sense of humor about the inevitable limitations of even the most ambitious and well-meaning efforts. There is much joy in seeing the good that can be done by various projects and yet the magnitude of the continuing challenges is staggering. "Despite many creative endeavors, there remains a huge and consistent underclass because new challenges are coming up all the time. For example, in the case of improving the quality of and access to water bodies, new negative externalities crop up, which undermine all the societal work that has been done," remarks Rohini.

At present, the size and scale of philanthropic response are so ill-matched to the scale of the problems India faces that it poses a quixotic challenge for those who want to engage in this sphere. Even as they push for more and more energy and funds in this sphere, they need to simultaneously remain fairly humble about being able to actually bring about change.

Above all, this highlights the fact that many problems, whether social, economic or ecological, cannot be solved by the influx of money alone. They require a greater input of not just skills but also political engagement by all of us as citizens.

In this context, Rohini feels an urgent need for more public platforms for discussion over issues or views that divide us. More often than not the public discourse appears sharply polarized with issues and concerns being presented in a stark manner without the nuances that actually make up everyday life.

This realization, coupled with an innate faith in the power of dialogue, led Rohini to design and compere the show *Uncommon Ground* on NDTV 24×7 in 2008. The eight episodes of this show brought together leaders from the corporate world and leaders from the social sector to discuss critical issues like health, energy, displacement and more. These conversations between individuals with diverse backgrounds, later brought out as a book, explored areas of convergence and disagreements between the for-profit and non-profit sectors while focusing on larger questions such as what kind of growth will really bring well-being for all.

Such experiences make the onward journey look simultaneously exciting and precarious. It is exciting because over the years, in diverse forums across the world, Rohini has found that many people feel a creative discontent over a fundamental question. Why is there such concentrated accumulation of wealth in the first place? What are the societal structures which allow some of us to remain this wealthy?

"Over the five to ten years, this question has become more alive than before and there is a global quest to seek answers. I do feel proud that Infosys created a model for an ethically grounded generation of completely white wealth. At the same time, I question what kind of social, economic and political structures allow such concentration," says Rohini thoughtfully.

The precariousness is related not just to the fuzzy and nebulous nature of these energies, but also to the staggering scale at which environmental degradation and disparity of economic opportunity are increasing. In this context, the emphasis on scale and impact of philanthropic endeavors often looks more and more like good intentioned bravado.

But, what a time to be alive! "It is a privilege to be part of the churn even though we don't know what will happen. What matters is that we have not only the power to act but also the *responsibility* to act. We can't just be consumers of systems that work for some of us, and even partially, we have to be co-creators of governance structures that will work for everyone," remarks Rohini on a positive note.

BIOGRAPHER

Rajni Bakshi is a Mumbai-based author who has spent the last three decades in the fertile ground between journalism and activism – chronicling struggles for more humane and ecologically sound ways of life. She is the author of *Bazaars, Conversations and Freedom: For a Market Culture Beyond Greed and Fear*, which has won two Vodafone-Crossword Awards. Her earlier book *Bapu Kuti: Journeys in Rediscovery of Gandhi* inspired the Hindi film *Swades,* directed by Ashutosh Gowarikar. Her other books include: *Long Haul: the Bombay Textile Workers Strike 1982-83* (1986), *A Warning and an Opportunity: the Dispute over Swami Vivekananda's Legacy* (1994), *LET'S Make it Happen: a Backgrounder on New Economics* (2003) and *Economics for Well-Being* (2007).

Modern education may make one intelligent but not wise. Wisdom comes from self-awareness, from our understanding of human values and from an active conscience. Such traits give us the social consciousness and independent will to choose right over wrong.

– Jeroninio

Go for Change

Gul Panag

Effervescent beauty, avid adventurer, relentless campaigner, fervent nature-lover, itinerant traveler, eloquent speaker – all these epithets describe Gul Panag, but, still do not do complete justice to her multi-faceted and many-layered personality. Most people know her as an 'actor who does intelligent films' and many also remember that she had won the Miss India crown in 1999. But, for Gul, the whole is greater than the sum of all parts. And way beyond and above the glamour and the stardust, her persona comprises a compassionate heart, a selfless spirit and a benevolent soul.

Born in Chandigarh in 1979 into the second generation of a family connected with the armed forces, Gul was exposed to many different places, cultures and influences on account of her father's frequent transfers. In an eloquent testimony to her versatility, Gul graduated in mathematics and did her master's in far-removed political science!

As a professional who has to rely upon her abilities to speak and deliver dialogues, public speaking comes naturally to her. And for good reason: she has been the winner of several state and national-level debating competitions, including two gold medals at the prestigious Annual National Inter-University Debate.

Entering the Miss India pageant, then, was a natural corollary to her many talents. It came as no surprise when she was crowned Miss India Universe in 1999, then still in her teens. However, the crown did not deter her from completing her B.A. (Mathematics) degree for which she took a sabbatical.

Gul has reached where she is today through hard work, passion and intelligence. After winning the crown, she did modelling assignments and television shows (including *Vijay Jyoti,* and the critically acclaimed *Kashmeer*). Finally, Gul graduated to her most natural vocation, cinema. And the list of her cinematic achievements is impressive. Her first film, *Dhoop,* was well-received, as were her award-winning portrayals of Zeenat in Nagesh Kukunoor's *Dor* and Nimmi in *Manorama Six Feet Under.*

Then came *Summer* 2007 directed by Suhail Tatari, where again, she earned rave reviews. *Hello,* her first big budget outing, met with a fair degree of success and her glamorous avatar in it took people by pleasant surprise, bringing appreciation from audiences and critics alike.

But after *Straight,* Gul got the unanimous and often-hard-to-get approval of all concerned. She became the favourite of the discerning and thinking audiences. Next seen as Nandita Sharma in Ram Gopal Verma's *Rann,* Gul proved her acting prowess by holding her own in an ensemble cast led by the one-and-only Amitabh Bachchan.

Her recent film *Turning 30,* proved to be another feather in her cap. The Prakash Jha venture got superlative reviews for her uninhibited portrayal of a modern woman defying stereotypes and living life on her own terms. The film further strengthened Gul's reputation for doing socially relevant movies. Her recently released film *Fatso* directed by Rajat Kapoor was a unique independent film.

Gul today stands at that threshold, where she is respected not just as an actor but also as a human being par excellence. And the road ahead is long, challenging and promising. What sets her apart from her contemporaries is the fact that she is a thinking actor and is choosy about the roles she accepts. She has steadfastly stayed away from the routine but commercially attractive song-and-dance roles and instead looks for 'characters' before she agrees to do a film.

She is particular about playing diverse characters, and works hard to make them look visually different from each other. Be it the short-haired Peehu of *Dhoop*, the glamorous Sonia in *Jurm*, the intense, sans make-up Zeenat in *Dor*, the nagging wife Nimmi in *Manorama Six Feet Under* or the yuppie Priyanka in *Hello* – all portray striking cameos. As she says, "I don't go by what others are doing. I opt for what I feel is right. We are gifted with brains and can choose for ourselves, so I chose characters that I could relate with and the characters that portrayed Indian women. I have never rated quantity over quality and will continue to do so." Gul's rather versatile and unusual looks also help her in playing diverse characters convincingly.

In fact, acting, central as it is to her life, is just one part of it. She is also an avid reader, often gorging through two to three books simultaneously, not surprisingly, they are strategically placed: one at her bedside, another in the car and a third one, usually in her handbag. She has a large collection of books, her library often being a mélange of first editions. Her literary interest is wide ranging as are her other passions. Gul's all-time favorite books include *A Wild Sheep Chase* by Haruki Murakami, *Atlas Shrugged* by Ayn Rand and the *Harry Potter* series.

Coming from a services background, love for sports is a natural corollary for her. For keeping in fine fettle, Gul turns to tennis and swimming. She is a keen rider as well. She's been riding from the age of ten and hasn't stopped since. As a young girl, she participated and won medals in various equestrian events. She makes sure that she takes time out of her busy schedule to indulge in her love for horses and riding.

That she is in fabulous shape is rather well known, but what is little known is that Gul has the spirit of steel and a remarkably tough core. She has amazingly high levels of endurance and strength as is clear from her track record of running marathons. She has run the Mumbai International Marathon every year since its inception and trains regularly to build and maintain her stamina. It is a tribute to Gul's nonchalance for glamour that when most actresses are caught-up with their looks, make-up and hair styles, Gul is remarkably unconcerned about these externalities when she runs the marathons in her track pants devoid of any make-up.

She also enjoys adventure and endurance sports such as white water-rafting, rock-climbing and trekking and takes time out of her busy schedule to indulge in them liberally.

She recently went hiking in the greater Himalayas and has come back enthralled. "These activities allow me to view my work and life in general from a new perspective each time," she avers. A roadie to boot, Gul has defied the traditional female stereotypes by owning a custom-made Scorpio 4by4 and the two can often be spotted exploring tracks in the nearby hills of Lonavala and Karnala. Driving from Mumbai to Leh (Ladakh) and camping on the way, has been an eagerly awaited annual pilgrimage for her for the last four years.

A keen shooter, Gul is also very good at handling guns and has been shooting skeet and rifle since her early teens. She often shoots with and trains under her brother Sherbir, a national-level shooter. Shooting helps her maintain focus and tests her concentration to its limits. Not unnaturally, she has set her sights on competitive shooting.

A hunger to visit new places often sees Gul taking off to lesser-known destinations. Her rationale is logical: the more she travels, the more she learns and absorbs in her persona, which in turn means that she can give more to each role that she portrays.

Her passion for traveling to off-beat places has been rewarding in more ways than one. 'Visit Finland' has appointed her their honorary brand ambassador in India. Her current agenda is to visit every single Wonder of the World (ancient as well as modern). Up next is a visit planned to the stone city of Petra in Jordan and lots more to Finland.

But, her quest for professional excellence has not dimmed her interest in serving society, working for the needy, being an instrument of positive change and giving back to the society and the environment. For a number of years, Gul has worked to raise funds and awareness for Shraddha, a school that rehabilitates young autistic adults. She has also lent her support to 'Shop For Change Fair Trade', a concern that promotes fair trade opportunities for poor cotton cultivators of Telengana, Vidarbha and Kutch, and 'Green Commandos', a citizen action initiative to save the environment.

She recently cemented her association with Sulabh International on World Health Day to work together to promote public health through sanitation. The NGO – Sulabh Shauchalya – sets up public toilets that provide affordable sanitation. To promote literacy, she embarked on a novel scheme that involved collecting used computers for installation at village schools and began a basic computer literacy program for the poor. In keeping with contemporary exigencies of minimizing the use of non-renewable resources, Gul is actively studying, promoting and installing practical solar and rain harvesting systems.

Gul's social consciousness has its genesis in the inspiration provided by her grandfather, Colonel Shamsher Singh, who was held in high esteem for being a good samaritan with an unblemished track record of working untiringly and selflessly for the welfare of others. Founded in his memory, the Colonel Shamsher Singh Foundation is an initiative to contribute to society, preserve the environment and extend help to the needy. The foundation chiefly comprises the Panag family as its trustees and Gul is its driving force.

According to Gul, "The Foundation facilitates bringing together public and private partnerships to promote inclusive development. We design programs with our partner NGOs and allow people an opportunity to work for the lesser privileged sections of society."

Gul 4 Change or G4C is a sub-program of the foundation. Through this platform, Gul is spearheading path-breaking social transformation in many fields, primarily gender equality and environment protection. Deeply concerned by the abysmally low sex ratio and rampant female feticide in Punjab, Gul has taken up cudgels to raise awareness about gender equality and eradicate these malpractices. For this, she works with established NGOs to promote their cause nationally and internationally, so that they are not short on funds and are able to make a difference.

The Foundation has tied up with the Union Territory (UT) administration to monitor the ultrasound centers in Chandigarh and convince pregnant women not to go in for female feticide. In an interview, Gul said her NGO will take the addresses of the women from these centers.

"We will work in tandem with the UT Health Department. Our volunteers will go to the homes of the women and generate awareness against female feticide. We will keep the complete database and follow up on their pregnancies. Our aim is to eradicate this discrimination against the girl child, though we know that we have a long way to go," she said.

The foundation is also actively working for gender equality in her home district Fatehgarh Sahib. As much as her professional life, Gul is equally passionate about the work being done by the foundation. She personally supervised a week-long awareness and signature campaign in Fatehgarh Sahib against female feticide. She parked herself at a local gurdwara in the township, urging people to pledge that they will not discriminate against their daughters or kill female fetuses. "I know all these signatures do not mean that these people will not indulge in female feticide now," Gul admits. "But, even if I plant the seed of the idea in them, the work will begin," she says with hope.

Gul has promised to visit her home district every month to work on major local issues like gender equality and awareness against drug addiction. "Punjab in general and Fatehgarh Sahib district in particular have the lowest sex ratio in the country. Female feticide here is amongst the highest in the world. In addition, we have a major problem of drug addiction, which is consuming Punjabi youth in large numbers. Our foundation is now working with established NGOs to address the issues in Punjab," she points out.

"I have found that at both the national and the international levels, people want to join hands and work for good causes. I am happy that I am able to reach out to people and form a link with the grassroots level, where change must come about," she says.

"We are tying up with schools and colleges across India to build a movement of students interested in the environment. We recently conducted a survey and found that nine out of ten students believe that something needs to be done about the environment," she says.

In the field of environment, G4C aggressively works with its volunteers, partner-NGOs and government bodies to promote basic sanitation, medical help, first aid, rainwater harvesting, tapping of solar and wind energy, public toilets and waste disposal.

Gul's ambit of concern includes disaster management and disaster preparedness as well. As a nation that is prone to all sorts of natural calamities, Gul feels that little has been done in this sphere. G4C has plans to have a list of volunteers who will be available for help as soon as a disaster strikes. G4C will ensure that these volunteers are trained and the teams are equipped and funded to act when required. Protocols and procedures will be established to achieve smooth operation as far as possible.

Yet another area where G4C is active is education and employment. Its endeavor is to arrest the alarming school drop-out rates by building partnerships between community-based NGOs and educational institutions. It also promotes vocational and practical education to address the problem of unemployment.

She is also the spokesperson for Social Outreach Accreditation Programme or SOAP, which is a free portal that brings together stakeholders involved in social engagement and mobilizes people for bringing the world together with volunteer work and community service and enables overall social health. It is Gul's attempt to create an environment that will throw up solutions to our problems. She believes that all of us can make efforts and adds, "If a million causes have a million supporters, the world will definitely be a better place to live in. Go ahead, pick a cause. Do your bit."

Gul quotes, "Looking back at my school years, two definitive non-academic programs stand out – The Duke of Edinburgh's Award at The Lawrence School, Lovedale and the mandatory 200 hours of community service I did during my A-levels at the International School of Lusaka, Zambia. Both were clearly laid out, transparent and instilled a sense of duty to give back to society at a very young age. Most importantly, they were recognized the world over. And since I was an early convert to the idea of community service, it is something I have tried to promote over the years. Social engagement, however, is easy to preach, but tough to implement in India, a country that probably needs it the most. The reason is the lack of a volunteering culture and also the lack of credible, transparent framework. Unlike in the West, where to get into graduate programs in top colleges, one has to have community service experience, here, sadly our universities don't put forth such prerequisites. Of course, there is the state-backed NSS, but like everything state-backed, it lacks passion and zeal."

Gul has leveraged the platform of Twitter rather intelligently for voicing her concerns and interacting with her fans, followers and like-minded people. As she says, "I view my job as an opportunity to get a platform to make people hear what I have to say and that's a much greater role to play for me. My professional life gives me a platform to reach people, and change and influence them. For me, that will be a far greater contribution than running around trees, singing songs," she says pithily.

So this is Gul Panag. One can only hope that her example will inspire more celebrities to leverage their fame and fan-following to effect change and ameliorate the lot of the underprivileged.

BIOGRAPHER

Sharmila Chandra is a former journalist and now works in the publishing industry. As a writer, her areas of interest include human rights, social trends and matters pertaining to children. She has written several human interest stories during her stint with The *Times of India* and *India Today.*

In a world that is becoming increasingly materialistic, we all need help to re-discover our purpose and invest in an egalitarian, humane and responsible society.

– Jeroninio

Everyone: A Changemaker

Bill Drayton

Listening to Bill Drayton is like quietly absorbing a subtle painting. Like a painter, he can see the world, including human beings, in great detail. His conversations unfold how the world works and where it is going. This gets through to you like a great painting does. The flow of hands while he speaks only adds to this experience. The softness of his delivery somehow underlines his clarity of thought, strong beliefs and optimism rooted in determination. His thought, mannerisms, and life story evoke the picture you have in your mind of Mahatma Gandhi.

Bill, one of the foremost thinkers of our time, founded the field of social entrepreneurship and its central organization, Ashoka: Innovators for the Public, in 1981. Ashoka now operates in more than 80 countries. Bill pioneered the concept of social entrepreneurs, differentiating them from the millions of social workers we have always had among us.

Born in New York City, Bill earned his bachelors from Harvard University in 1965 and his masters from Balliol College, Oxford University, in 1967. In 1970, Bill received a law degree from Yale University and an honorary doctorate from Yale University in 2009. These years are important. The sequence of events during this period in the US built the foundation of social entrepreneurship on which Bill operates. In elementary school, Bill launched and ran a series of newspapers. He built the Asia Society in high school, which he nurtured lovingly to make it the largest student

31

organization. In high school and at Harvard, he engaged in and was deeply moved by the civil rights movement. The fact that it was a Gandhian movement drew him closer to India and, indeed, to several leading Gandhians in India.

From his school years, Bill carried forward a love for creating things for the good, closeness to nature rooted in his love of backpacking and commitment to service enriched by India and Mahatma Gandhi.

As a 20-year-old, Bill drove a car from Munich to India to explore the country. While in India, he spent several weeks with Vinoba Bhave, the spiritual successor to Gandhi and leader of the immensely successful Bhoodan Movement. Bill, who had been an entrepreneur since he was in fifth grade, came to regard Vinoba as a remarkable social entrepreneur as well as a spiritual force. Vinoba and his constructive workers convinced millions of village landowners to donate part of their land to their poorer neighbors. Bill was deeply moved to see the tremendous power of a social entrepreneur armed with a simple idea. Before Vinoba's death, seven million acres of land had been gifted by landowners to the socially and economically weaker sections of the society.

In Vinoba and others, Bill could see the impact of an entrepreneur powered by an idea and driven by the vision to bring about large-scale change. He resolved to work with such people across the world.

Bill formed Ashoka in 1980. Its first objective and still the organization's bedrock work is to find the most important new ideas that have the potential to benefit others, in the hands of the best social entrepreneurs wherever they are in the world, help launch them and continue to help them in their endeavor for life. Bill patiently and persistently built a movement of thousands of volunteers and also funders, writers and others. He convinced them that these people needed to be looked at from the lens of an entrepreneur. Just like a business entrepreneur, a social entrepreneur seizes an opportunity and comes out with an innovative idea and ventures to execute the same for the betterment of people.

India was the first country where Bill and the Ashoka Board Members came to look for Ashoka Fellows. These Fellows are chosen because they are change-makers who want to make a difference in society. Gloria de Souza from Mumbai was selected as one of the first Ashoka Fellows. Gloria, a teacher in an elementary school, was not happy with the rote method of learning that her children were being forced to use. It pained her to hear children reading out nursery rhymes that had references to flowers, plants and animals that the children had never seen. She created a new method of teaching that connected the children to the world they belonged to and that encouraged them to be creative, hands-on problem-solvers. A true social entrepreneur, she quit teaching to launch *Parisar Asha,* an organization that has spread her idea to schools across India and beyond. Gloria is today credited with the introduction of Environmental Science (EVS) classes in thousands of schools. In the words of Bill, "There is nothing more powerful than a new idea – if it is in the hands of a true entrepreneur."

When someone asked Bill to define social entrepreneurship, he said: "In a crisis, it is sometimes necessary to give people fish; generally it is better to teach them to fish; but the real leverage is to change the nature and structure of the fishing industry."

Ashoka elects leading social entrepreneurs and provides them with financial support for an average of three years to allow them to devote themselves fully for the launch of their entrepreneurial ventures. However, the membership of the Ashoka fellowship is for life. The biggest value of being elected an Ashoka Fellow is to be invited into the richly active community of 3,000 peer top social entrepreneur fellows across the world. The fellowship is sector agnostic and is offered to social entrepreneurs in every space one can imagine.

Ashoka has developed a rigorous five-step selection process that chooses leading social entrepreneurs who have the capability to create very significant, at least continental-scale social change. The most important of these criteria is the uniqueness of the solution. To be considered for the fellowship, it is essential that the social entrepreneurs have the most innovative of solutions to address an issue. Ashoka then looks for the possibility of the solution-changing patterns in the space it is being implemented. "Will it change its fishing industry?" An election also requires the person to be highly creative, have top entrepreneurial quality and have exceptional ethical fiber.

This process works. More than 50 percent of the Ashoka Fellows have changed national policies within five years of their launch. Over three-quarters have changed the patterns of their fields nationally within the same period. The statistics have remained steady over 10 years of evaluation and also across the world's continents.

The first step to becoming a social entrepreneur, Bill will tell you, is to give yourself the permission to be one. Many people care about social problems. Some even have innovative solutions. However, it is only a social entrepreneur who decides to apply those solutions, experiment, be prepared for failure and ridicule and yet persist. Social entrepreneurs carry a larger vision of changing the world. Their ideas have the power to upset existing arrangements.

"The most powerful force in the world is a pattern changing idea – if it is in the hands of a serious social entrepreneur," says Bill. One of the best examples of social entrepreneurs Bill often cites is that of Florence Nightingale.

As a nurse during the Crimean War, Florence was moved by the high rate of mortality in the military hospitals. She decided to dig deeper into the cause of the problem. It did not take her too long to learn that the primary reason was the poor hygienic conditions that war victims had to endure. She put in place several steps to improve these conditions in the hospitals, which reduced the death rate from 40 percent to 2 percent. Like a true social entrepreneur, Florence learned that her experience at the Crimean War was an idea that had the potential to change her 'fishing industry'. She dedicated the rest of her life to building the new profession of nursing, bringing revolutionary changes to the pedagogy of nursing and introducing innovative processes to alleviate suffering of the patients. She did not rest until the medical fraternity, and not just the British Army, adopted the modernization of the nursing sector. Today's nursing practices the world has adapted owe much to Florence.

The strength of the fellowship lies in its active network. Today, the 3,000 Ashoka Fellows, spread across 80 countries, have the power to share knowledge, help one another and collaborate to create much bigger impact across geographies. Each of them is a thought-leader in his/her chosen space and geography. Bill's vision of supporting leading social entrepreneurs in their journey takes shape through the fellowship.

Bill and his team at Ashoka realized that something more powerful than social entrepreneurship takes place when entrepreneurs come together. Bill calls it 'collaborative entrepreneurship'. When the team identifies the work of an Ashoka Fellow moving towards creating pattern change, it works with the fellow to create a global team of teams that includes other stakeholders, including business entrepreneurs. Players in this team then collaborate to realize the new paradigm faster.

Over the last two years, Bill's team has successfully implemented the collaborative entrepreneurship model in the field of affordable housing in India. In its first 14 months, it built or had under construction 15,000 new homes for urban informal sector workers with ₹ 120 million of private finance. Citizen-groups do the local work and business does the development, building and finance. This business/social team of teams is now working on various projects from city to city because everyone benefits greatly.

Responding to a question from eBay founder, Pierre Omidyar, eight years ago, Bill and Ashoka President Emeritus, Sushmita Ghosh, recognized that Ashoka's central goal had to become more explicit – helping the world become an 'Everyone a Changemaker' society. That realization, in turn, clarified and greatly sharpened Ashoka's approach, its organization and the movement it leads.

That Bill and Ashoka responded so easily and adapted so significantly is a good example of one of the important things that sets entrepreneurs apart. "They do not 'get an idea' and then 'go and implement it'. The entrepreneurial path is one of constantly creating, listening, experimenting and creating again," he says.

The change Bill envisages here is as profound as any in history. It is the shift from a world organized around repetition (where the pieces fit together as each keeps doing the same thing) to a world organized around the opposite principle – change (where each change causes change in those around it, which in turn begets further change).

What is forcing this extraordinary transformation? "The rate at which change is escalating is exponential. So is the increase in the number of changemakers and perhaps, most importantly in the combinations, and the combinations of combinations of changemakers. That's the central fact and driving force of this era. We can't stop it. It's a fact." (Bill, at Harvard Business School, February 2012)

Bill argues in speech after speech that these ever more powerful and ever more pervasive forces of change are breaking down the world of repetition. The institutions that characterize this world were designed for efficiency in repetition. Their limited nervous system runs from the few managers downward. They are divided and set apart by walls.

Instead, in a world defined by change, the world must be organized in highly fluid teams of teams. Value will increasingly come from understanding and contributing to a world of fluid, fast-moving change. The institutions of the past, increasingly, simply are unable to cope with, let alone compete, in this radically different world.

Teams require everyone to be a player and in this world to be a player, one must be able to contribute to change, which requires everyone to develop new skills. This in turn requires a new paradigm of what success means in growing up and in education.

Bill and Ashoka were moving towards this future intuitively earlier. However, over the last half-a-dozen years, this new clarity has been transformative. Launching, helping succeed and weaving together the world's most powerful new ideas and entrepreneurs for the good of all remain the foundation of their work. However, they are now also powerfully organized to help the world reach through the tipping process to its 'everyone a changemaker' future.

There are 700 leading social entrepreneur Ashoka fellows across the world (out of 3,000) focused on children and young people. Looking at their highly successful, pattern-changing work, Bill and Ashoka have been able to define the new paradigm for growing up.

In the world of repetition, mastering a body of knowledge and a set of rules was enough for a successful life. One simply applied that skill set and dealt with others by following a settled set of rules. That is, therefore, what school principals and pretty much everyone else in the educational system is held accountable for – test results and the discipline of the pupils.

However, that definition is utterly inadequate today. As Bill pointed out very early, "Any young child who does not master the skill of empathy at a high level will be marginalized and thrown out in life." He adds, "As the rate of change accelerates, and as we are thrown together in ever more unpredictable and diverse ways, the rules cover less and less. Anyone who does not guide himself/herself with great empathetic skills and therefore ethics will hurt others and disrupt groups. They will be thrown out and no one will care about their knowledge, even if it is computer science."

Once one understands this, it is easy to grasp why Bill is so deeply committed to introducing the new paradigm – that every single child must master empathy. "To deny anyone the right to be a part of society and to contribute love and respect at the highest possible level is the cruelest and destructive thing one can do to another person." Here, one can palpably feel his deep-rooted sense of civil rights and Gandhian perspective.

Among them, the 700 fellows have demonstrated how to do this quickly, inexpensively and effectively.

Mary Gordon, a Canadian Ashoka fellow, for example, has shown how young children who have not been given the skill of empathy at home, in the street, or in school can and will grasp it in 20-plus hours. Bullying rates come down and stay down. Her work has now spread across three continents. How does she do this? The heart of her approach is an infant who at the beginning of the school year, is typically in the 2- to 4-month-old range. The infant, accompanied by his mother or occasionally father, comes to the first or third grade classroom once a month for an hour. The infant, wearing a T-shirt labeled 'The Professor', presides from atop a green blanket. The first-graders or third-graders have the responsibility of figuring out what the professor is saying and then feeling. They also absorb the very high empathy level between the professor and their accompanying parents.

Another Ashoka fellow has restored recess by restructuring it around group-play which, of course, is a rich opportunity for children to practice empathy. Others have achieved the same result in the classroom or have focused on fifth to eighth grade girls who tend to lose self-confidence and become "mean girls".

Once you know what you are looking for, then the challenge is not in knowing how to solve the problem or how to remove the chief cause of marginalization and prejudice. It is, instead, in changing the world's framework of thinking the definition of what success in growing up is.

Here Bill has thrown himself into the challenge of how to tip the world's thinking and, in the process, help develop the methodology for the field for all the other changes that are needed.

The heart of this new approach is a global team of teams using Ashoka's revolutionary collaborative entrepreneurship approach. To tip the world, there are ten key places that are critical. For example: India, Indonesia, Brazil and the US. Bill and Ashoka's strategy in each is to do what every entrepreneur must always do – to set in motion powerful forces that will pull society to a new and better place, forces far bigger than any the entrepreneur can bring to bear directly.

Here is how, using the US as an example, this will happen. A team of Ashoka fellows (including Mary) with the Ashoka staff is recruiting 60 schools that represent the country's enormous diversity to take a lead. Each school has a track record of leading change and, in each case, has an internal team that tries to reach the 'Every Child Must Master Empathy' goal. The team of fellows and Ashoka encourage these school-based teams, connect them with one another, connect them with the methods developed by the 700 fellows worldwide, and be in touch through Ashoka's www.changemakers.com to anyone anywhere in the world who wants to bring the benefits of this change to their children and to contribute to the broader effort. Each school-based team entrepreneurs its way to its own success and contributes whatever it learns to the global team of teams thus created.

Also, Ashoka is building relationships with roughly 30 of the most thoughtful writers and publishers in each of the ten key regions of the world.

By year three, probably 50 of the original 60 schools in America would have succeeded and would be on fire to spread the word. The Ashoka team then connects the writers and publishers who understand how critical it is for the future of their country to move quickly to its 'everyone a changemaker' future to the schools. Soon parents will be asking principals: "How good is your school at empathy?"

Policy-makers will not be far behind. The tipping process will be underway.

The same broad approach applies to the other major changes needed to reach the 'everyone a changemaker' future: A global team of teams with collaborative entrepreneurship across hundreds of the world's leading entrepreneurs in the area. Each resulting change contributes a key part of the architecture of the world of change that is now upon us.

Bill Drayton's life is dedicated to the cause of building a world that is ever ready for newer challenges. He saw that social entrepreneurs are pivotal in creating such a world. For the last 30 years, he has mastered the processes to find them around the world and then to support them in their venture and in getting them to collaborate. He now believes that the world has reached the turning point where it is both possible and essential for every one of the earth's inhabitants to be a changemaker. He continues to inspire an entire new generation to think differently about their role as citizen changemakers in the world. He remarks that, "For any country to succeed in a world defined by change, an 'everyone a changemaker' world, all its young children must master a high level of empathetic skill and every teen must be a changemaker, because practice is the only way to succeed."

Author David Bornstein in his book *How to Change the World: Social Entrepreneurs and the Power of New Ideas,* quotes one of Bill's college professors describing Bill as having 'the determination of Steve Jobs and the brains of a Nobel laureate.'

BIOGRAPHER

Manoj Chandran was until recently the director of Framework Change function at Ashoka Innovators for the Public, where he was responsible for leveraging the powerful platform of social entrepreneurs to develop inclusive communication strategies that provide citizens opportunities to go through change making experiences. Manoj has several years of marketing and communications experience, having headed corporate marketing function at MindTree and served as technology and business journalist.

Today, the need of the hour is to move from social entrepreneurship to NOBLE entrepreneurship, where instead of prioritizing on profits, our larger focus should be on our passion and commitment to make a difference to our planet and people.

– Jeroninio

Son to a Million Parents

Sailesh Mishra

Deshamma Kutty (name changed on request) lay dying in Sailesh's arms. "Don't worry, mother," he whispered softly in her ear, stroking her bald pate reassuringly. "We will meet again when you are reborn," he said. Deshamma burst into a smile and closed her beady eyes, for the last time. "I will perform the last rites," declared Sailesh, shocked but serene, through his tears. Deshamma's one and only son had declined to be by his mother's side in her last moments at the old-age home, where Sailesh volunteered. He had earned the status of the residents' universal son.

If Sailesh Mishra has today become the son-figure to India's ageing population, estimated at 96 million in 2011, it is not merely because of his uncanny knack for forging a personal bond with elderly individuals across caste, community and region. It's more because of over the past 20 years, he has woven intricate and widespread networks of people, issues and solutions, which have collectively created reassurance and hope for the elders in the country. His mission is to put a smile on every face that looks at the sunset with the foreboding of the inevitable end.

A program on senior citizens, telecast in 2004, on Sahyadri TV, the government-run channel in Marathi, made Sailesh sit up. The next morning, he found himself knocking at the door of Dignity Foundation, one of the NGOs that had participated in the program. He offered to be a volunteer, but received a job offer, as he was found

43

brimming with ideas. This was the beginning of his tryst with elders. He began afresh with a 75 percent cut in the salary he drew in the corporate world, and with an enormous hope of finding his calling. The next eight years were marked by his single-minded drive to fulfill this hope. "Through the severe financial hardship we faced during this phase, my wife Mona and daughter Drishti were my steadfast partners and eternal sources of support," he says.

The Dignity Foundation assigned to Sailesh the management of 11 centers of senior citizen identity cards, issued by the government of Maharashtra via NGOs, to people who are over 60 years of age. This card enables them to avail of certain concessions and benefits from the public as well as private sectors. It normally takes 60 to 90 days for an ID card to be issued. Sailesh was well equipped for such a managerial role. For a senior citizen, who was in urgent need, Sailesh did some running around and secured the card for him within 60 days. As he handed over the card, the man blessed Sailesh by placing his palms on his head. The next moment the man fished out of his pocket a Ravalgaon candy that cost 25 paisa in those days, and placed it on Sailesh's palm. Overwhelmed by this simple experience, Sailesh's attention now came to rest on a new aspect of his passion for people: the crucial role of personal care and attention. He began to crave the satisfaction he derived from such encounters.

Soon enough, an opportunity presented itself. The post of vice president of the Neral township for senior citizens, the dream project of Dignity Foundation, fell vacant and Sailesh opted to take responsibility, as he had previous experience of working with architects and engineers. He was appointed chief of the project still under construction and was required to visit it twice a week, which took his total daily commute to 180 km. He often worked for over 16 hours a day, multi-tasking with architects, planners, construction workers, local politicians, residents, government officials, lawyers, NGOs and the police, happy to be able to contribute, enjoying every moment of his demanding schedule. But, he was hardly home and his family life was in a shambles. As the work at the township picked up the pace, Sailesh moved lock, stock and barrel to the site, going home only once a month.

His stay at the township gave him deep insights into the life of elders and took him to the next step, much beyond the heavy workload of marketing and administrative responsibility, into the realm of profoundly moving human relationships. Sailesh accomplished a lot of work online since communication lines were feeble at Neral. "Here I learned the magic of Internet and the basic knowledge of aging and dementia, which sowed the seeds of my future foray into the global forum of elder care," he recalls.

When the arrival of the first resident was announced, the whole township went into a tizzy, as nothing was quite ready. Taking a leadership role, Sailesh rushed against time with furniture and fittings, paint and polish, upholstery and wiring, and set up one cottage within three days. With such a state of affairs, Sailesh not only grew exceptionally sensitive to the needs of elders, but also learnt to pacify them when things were far from perfect. Families who left their elders at the township came to trust Sailesh. They saw that he got up in the middle of the night to attend to their needs with a smile. Aggrieved residents would listen to nobody but Sailesh.

He got the shock of his life when he found an 86-year-old lady demanding to go to school. "What school?" he laughed and dismissed the demand but she was persistent.

After some time he began to take her every day to a make-believe school within the township, and bring her back, a satisfied 'schoolgirl'. The strangeness of the demand and the simplicity of the solution left a niggling question mark in his mind.

Another lady, frail and docile, made Sailesh sing the same song every night, and would sleep only after she had heard it. Every encounter with a resident taught Sailesh that beyond administrative efficiency and technological advancement, it was essential to be a human being.

One morning, a horrified attendant came running to Sailesh holding the shower head that this lady had uprooted from the bathroom. This was Sailesh's first brush with the destructive power of dementia. And then he remembered the old man in a day care center: he wore diapers, danced and sang all day, played on the mouth organ and kept kissing everybody in sight. This man and many others were kept confined behind a collapsible grill, in jail-like conditions. Sailesh had found this cruel and irrational, but he could find no explanation. "How can we be so irrational and cruel to our elders, I wondered," says Sailesh. "I was intrigued and disturbed, but clueless," he adds.

Sleepless with puzzlement and anxiety, Sailesh ransacked the Internet and to his dismay found that it provided little help in dealing with the issues of elders. There was no information on old-age homes, NGOs, retirement plans, laws protecting the elders, day-care facilities, medical and healthcare issues and recreational needs. Restless and annoyed, Sailesh began to identify and listed the gaps – medical, financial, social and psychological – in the elder-care domain and aspired to bridge them. Since then, he has built, and continues to build, bridge after bridge between people, issues and solutions.

The first hand experience at the Neral township equipped Sailesh with multi-tasking skills, a holistic approach, technological prowess, the ability to deal with crisis situations and most importantly, an understanding of the need of the elders for the human touch. It laid the foundation for his leap forward from the cocoon of a person-centric approach into the macro space of geriatric research. Sailesh now decided to be on his own and placed his experience and expertise in the service of elders.

Treating the dearth of information as the first priority, Sailesh started off by sourcing articles on social issues for his blog peopleforsocialcause.com, which recorded 1,10,000 hits within four years. With characteristic perseverance, he started learning about search engine optimization, traffic, design and other tricks of the social media trade. Bhavesh Chheda, the website designer, became an ardent activist and close associate of Sailesh. Sailesh's fund-raising and marketing inputs for the Mumbai Mobile Crèche project helped establish him as a consultant on the social sector. He connected with karmayoga@yahoogroup, the most respected online community for social sector, and studied a wide range of causes across the country. It opened for him floodgates of information, knowledge and opportunities to build bridges and soon established him as a resource person and consultant on domains ranging from female feticide to rainwater harvesting to disability to vermiculture. Karmayoga worked wonders for him in the coming years.

Bhavesh helped Sailesh progress from the peopleforsocialcauses blog to a one-stop website for elders, which Sailesh named SilverInnings.com by consensus. Sailesh also started making his own original contribution to the website, which became a platform for sharing material on elder abuse, recreation, healthcare, diet, law, pension policies and many such issues.

SilverInnings.com could thus address the problem of information paucity, but eventually got sucked into the huge vacuum of services paucity. The website was inundated with queries regarding services for the elderly, leading to the setting up of Silver Innings Foundation (SIF) within three months. A modest 25 invites on April 10, 2008, for the launch of Silver Innings as a social enterprise, drew in over 350 people, mostly from Karmayoga, a sizeable constituency in his support. For this venture, Sailesh once again did what he is best at: he built bridges with inspiring people.

He brought on his panel his Paris-based Indian origin ex-colleague Hendi Lingiah, a French clinical psychologist having transnational experience and expertise in working with the elderly. Parul Kibliwalla, professor of nursing at L.T. College of Nursing (and his colleague from the Alzheimer's and Related Disorder Society of India) too joined him at Silver Innings. Dr P Vyasamoorthy, Founder President of the Society for Serving Seniors (SSS), Secunderabad and SSS Global, and a recent Karamveer Chakra Awardee teamed up as advisor. The nine trustees came from widely divergent areas: a chemical engineer, a website designer, two marketing experts, a nurse and a school teacher: all gerontologists in the age bracket of 26-45 years, addressing various needs of elders.

"I was moved to tears on reading issues about elders," says Bhavesh Chheda, website designer and the youngest member of the team. "I had no idea the field was so vast and required such urgent attention, until I read about it while designing the website. Sailesh has been a fountainhead of inspiration for me," he adds.

Parul Kibliwala, a professor of nursing at L.T. College of Nursing (SNDT), at 51, is the oldest member of Sailesh's team. She is also active with ARDSI's Mumbai chapter. "I saw Sailesh's irrepressible energy and zeal, and couldn't keep myself away," she says. "I am happy that my 20 years' experience in the nursing field has now been harnessed into his excellent work," she adds.

UnLtd India, the seed funding agency for change-makers, found the ideas presented SIF acceptable, and provided a token amount of ₹ 60,000 for the first level of funding, which took care of the administrative expenses. But more important were the non-monetary gains such as mentoring, shaping of the fledgling organization's ideas, hand-holding and nurturing. SIF was made to craft a vision, mission and objective statement, which sharpened the focus while boot camps, workshops and training sessions inducted professionalism into the work. SIF suddenly found itself posited on an international forum, surrounded by takers for their ideas. Another significant gain was Silver Inning's exposure to youth pursuing a broad spectrum of social ideas, which brought young inspiring people together in a rich process of cross-pollination.

UnLtd (pronounced unlimited) India also established the Hub in Bandra, Mumbai, which for the first time, gave to SIF a table space and an office address of its own. Activists met here to plan their campaigns and strategies, creating a vibrant, motivating and constructive environment of like-minded people. This greatly elevated the status of SIF. The tie-up was an endorsement of Silver Inning's vision, which emphasized that elders do not need charity but social enterprise.

In 2009, iCONGO, a citizens' movement that aims at sensitizing and creating awareness among people about socio-political issues, and at building individual social responsibility created a special category of Karmaveer national award for elder care and Sailesh was selected for receiving it, among ten others who represented various causes. This brought Sailesh the seed funding, an abundance of opportunities and loads of confidence. "I was enabled to network with like-minded people from areas other than aging, which was very enlightening and enriching," reveals Sailesh. "It opened a platform for long-term relationship through which our organizations could expand fund-raising and resource mobilization workshops for NGOs," he adds. As a result of this multifaceted collaboration, a Karmaveer Chakra was jointly launched in 2011, as a National Award to promote exceptional work in Elder Care.

Earlier, at an international conference on gerontology in Tirupati, convened by the one and only research institute on ageing in India, Sailesh was invited by director Prof R. Ramamurthy to speak on technolgy intervention for the elderly. In the presence of the global who's who, Sailesh delivered his highly acclaimed talk, opening the door for the entirely untapped area of networking and advocacy for elders through social media. This was an idea spectacularly ahead of its times. Sailesh also proposed an online resource library on ageing in India. Sailesh, while chairing a session at Tirupati on fighting for the rights of the aged, voiced a demand for a separate ministry for elder care. "Senior bureaucrats sitting here in this assembly must resign," he thundered to the dismay of the delegates, "as they have failed to implement the National Policy on Older People!" His passion and outspokenness on this occasion, earned him a nomination from Professor Joseph Troisi, Director of United Nations Institute of Ageing, to visit Malta on a 15-day course on gerontology.

On January 14, 2009, Sailesh suffered a heart attack while delivering a lecture and had to undergo angioplasty. Within a matter of 40 days, he had to leave for Malta, and it was his indomitable will that permitted him the travail. Sailesh has the honor of being the only person nominated by Professor Joseph Triosi twice to visit Malta.

In February 2009, Sailesh was in Malta to attend a course on social gerontology. "The international exposure, networking and the academic knowledge I gained in this first visit to Malta played a major role in speeding up my recovery," he smiles.

In October 2010, Sailesh revisited Malta on Prof Triosi's special recommendation, for taking a course on the implementation of the Madrid International Plan of Action on Ageing (MIPAA), widely considered the bible for ageing in the world. Sailesh was the only non-government person to have attended the MIPAA course. "MIPAA is a core document of UN on ageing, which demands that the governments of the world make policies and programs for elders," informs Sailesh. "This course gave me the advocacy tooth to fight for elders' rights within the government and the civil society," he says.

In January 2009, SNDT University asked SIF to partner an international conference as resource for providing topics and speakers. This symbolized Sailesh's triumphant entry into the academic world. In 2011, SIF was accredited as an NGO by the Second Session of the Open-Ended Working Group on Ageing (OEWGA) at the United Nations Program on Ageing, New York, from August 01 to 04, 2011. The SIF is also part of the international forum 'NGO Sub Committee to Promote a Human Rights Convention' since 2010, and a member of International Federation of Ageing (IFA) and International Network for Prevention of Elder Abuse (INPEA).

While creating impact and awareness, Sailesh's relentless work and the international fame he received spawned more work, which brought with it a lot of responsibility. Youth from the corporate world came for advice on where and how to help a social cause. SIF strongly protested against three dialogues in the Hindi film *Singh is King,* which insulted senior citizens, and the makers of the film were compelled to apologize for the offensive lines. SIF has filed petitions and written to the government on elder abuse, including murders of elders, dementia and other issues of the elderly. SIF also facilitated the S.P. Jain Social Impact Award.

Sailesh's robust optimism and never say die positivity keep him well supplied with innovative ideas for integration of the elders into the mainstream society. From parties to picnics and contests to games and sports, he has got elders on their feet dancing, singing, playing and enjoying every moment of life. He brought over 1,000 senior citizens to sing the national anthem and this feat was recorded in the Limca Book of Records. Following this achievement, Limca Book of Records had agreed to create a separate category for senior citizens.

The Umang talent show for the elderly, essay competitions for school children based on elders, World Elder Abuse Awareness Day programs in schools and a facilitator's role in the sports day program for the elderly conducted by FESCOM are all Sailesh's brainchildren. Recently, he got 100 elders dancing as a flash mob on the Bollywood hit song Chikni Chameli!

To cope with the burgeoning workload, Sailesh has erected a model on the twin pillars of teamwork and dissemination. Through this model, SIF has emerged as a major agent of change. As a social enterprise, SIF undertakes or promotes a self-sustaining commercial activity and ploughs the profits back into the cause. Like-minded individuals and organizations act as nodes that link up and network to enrich each other, with knowledge and experience while keeping the autonomy of each unit intact. It is a unique participatory model that has evolved through a vibrant sharing of ideas, experiences and collective wisdom.

Sailesh aims at converting the Silver Innings website into an e-commerce portal, with 25 percent of the earnings diverted towards the SIF. Rather than setting up multiple centers, SIF has tied up with domestic like-minded organizations like Helpage India, Harmony for Silvers Foundation, the Family Welfare Agency, FESCOM, AISCCON, Nightingale Trust, ARDSI, SNDT University, TISS, ILC-I, GSI, AGI, Times Foundation, HELP Library and many others for a democratic and collaborative approach to ageing. A refreshing 25 percent of SIF members are below the age of 30 years, hence a remarkably farsighted design that sensitizes youth to the needs of elders, channelizes the young generation's creative energy into a socially responsible activity and integrates the two distant age groups into a wholesome relationship has been developed. SIF has instituted an award for youth in the service of elders.

Thanks to Sailesh's involvement in so many causes, the civil society is awakening to the realities of elders' lives. Media involvement has also increased. Optimum use of social media has drawn in hordes of youth to the cause of elders. Several individual seniors have benefited directly or indirectly. Helpage India has started a social media initiative. Mumbai Marathon has extracted elders from the 'Other' category and created an independent one. The American Association for Retired People Global (AARP Global) has updated its India section after SIF asked them to do so. With open-mindedness and an accommodative approach, Sailesh has brought diverse individuals and organizations on a single platform, the success of which became obvious on August 16, 2010, collectively observed as a national protest day against elder abuse.

Sailesh was invited by the UN to participate in the third session of the prestigious 'Open-ended Working Group on Ageing' (OEWG) from August 21 to 24, 2012. In December 2011, he became the first South Asian to be featured on the renowned international USA-based radio station 'Alzheimer's Speaks Radio™'. On July 15, 2012, Sailesh participated in the *Satyamev Jayate* episode on senior citizens, a unique and very popular talk show hosted by Bollywood superstar Aamir Khan on Star Plus TV channel. The *Satyamev Jayate* team had invited Sailesh and SIF as partners, experts and a resource organization.

On August 17, 2013, he launched A1 Snehanjali, an assisted living elder care home under the Silver Innings banner, with a mission to transform the lives of elders by mitigating loneliness, helplessness and boredom and by helping them to live with dignity in their silver years.

Thus, Sailesh has ignited and activated the dormant ageing sector to create an environment and an understanding of ageing as a positive and beautiful experience with no negative adage to it.

And yet, Sailesh has a long wish-list. He wants to create a cadre of individuals in geriatric care and gerontology. He wants to set up training centers and build knowledge bases in this field. He wants to start a curriculum in gerontology offering short-term courses in or through existing universities and institutes for professionals and students. "We must set up a geriatric psychological service, equipped with a team of clinical psychologists, who will pay home visits to Alzheimer's patients. We must have talking clocks, bold font calendars, day reminders and other products needed by elders for sale in every neighborhood store. We can develop a replicable training module that can be used at the national level. We should try to devise ways and means of empowering the elderly to gain skill sets that could help them in successful and productive ageing. And... Oh, well, the sky is the limit!" he exclaims.

So what is Sailesh's dream-come-true? In his own words:

"SIF must cease to exist after 20 years, as the mainstream society will take on all its roles and functions. Product and service providers for elders will do brisk business in a thriving market. Above all, there will be no tears in the eyes of a dying elder."

BIOGRAPHER

Shubha Khandekar has been a journalist, writer, editor and cartoonist for the past 25 years. She has translated three books from Marathi into English and has written a book on ancient Indian history and a period novel.

I believe that everyone is a hero, a leader, a volunteer, a teacher and a champion of change. All we need to do is acknowledge and understand this and then help others to understand the same. That's all it takes to be a champion of change.

– Jeroninio

A Journey of a Thousand Miles Begins with a Single Step

Michael Norton

The Guardian refers to Michael Norton as a *'one-man idea factory'*. He is that and much more. Michael has spent his life generating ideas and putting them into action, while encouraging a lot of people to do the same.

What makes him do that? Michael says, "You can change the world with your wallet (your money), or with your diary (your time). But the best way to do so is with your brain (your ideas) and your energy and commitment."

A while ago, I was working in Bangladesh and was deeply influenced by Nobel Peace Prize recipient Muhammad Yunus and his ideas of micro-finance and financial self-sufficiency. I wished to do something on similar lines and that's how Michael and I met.

Michael had been supporting a competition in schools sponsored by CitiBank. Students had to speak on the subject of financial literacy. A popular topic that many students chose for their talk was *'Needs and Wants'*. What they said almost always went something like this: "These are my needs and these are my wants. Now that I understand the difference between *needs* and *wants*, I will spend my money on my needs. But, I will think carefully before spending on my wants. In this way, I will keep out of debt and start to save for my future."

Michael felt that this was a bit like telling young people to 'Just say no to drugs' and expect them to stay away from them. He knew this was just not enough motivation for the youth to become financially literate. The solution was to help them set up and run their very own bank at their school!

56

Michael knew that raising money even for the simplest of projects was a challenge faced by the youth. This impeded their understanding of financial matters and discouraged the development of their entrepreneurial skills. He wanted to encourage students to save, and also to be able to borrow small sums of money for projects they wanted to undertake. These projects could be as simple as running a disco to raise money for charity or mounting a photo exhibition. The small amount of money they needed to get started would be repaid out of money generated by the project. He wanted to find an enthusiastic young person, who was able and willing to take this idea forward and this is how I came to start MyBnk. With Michael's support and encouragement, I took MyBnk from an idea to a successful project. In doing this, I became a Young Social Entrepreneur of the Year in 2008, an Ashoka Fellow in 2010 and a World Economic Forum's Global Young Leader in 2011.

Michael believes that there are many young people with entrepreneurial talent, who want to change the world, and are just looking for a big idea to invest their time and energy in.

As Michael says, "I wanted to create a hands-on way for young people to learn about finance so that they could make more informed decisions on matters which could affect their future lives."

He was born into a privileged background. After winning a scholarship to Cambridge University and graduating with a science degree, like many young people starting out on their career, he was not sure about what he wanted to do. On his father's suggestion, he went into banking. His father also suggested that he volunteer as a youth leader, as his father was one when he was young.

Michael believes in 'trigger points'. As he explains in his book *The Everyday Activist,* "There are points in your life when you can decide to do something instead of doing something else or nothing at all. This could be when you meet and talk to someone, or hear about an idea, or see a simple statistic (such as a figure for the gender imbalance in India), and make a decision one way instead of another that could change the whole course of your future life. It did for me. My trigger point was my decision to volunteer."

Michael spent his Monday evenings at a youth club, organizing activities and initiating discussions with young people. He got some of them to visit old people in their homes. One evening, two teenaged girls came up to him with broad smiles on their faces. He asked them the reason for their smiles. The girls said that they had just taken an old person out to the shops. Michael asked them what was so extraordinary about this. The girls told him that the old woman hadn't left her flat in two years. The girls had borrowed a wheelbarrow, put some cushions in it, carried her down the stairs, and wheeled her to the shops, which no one had thought of doing!

The old woman had had an army of social workers and health visitors who looked after her. But, none of them had done anything about the fact that she was completely housebound. The two young people had found a simple solution! This is the essence of social entrepreneurship – thinking up a solution and then doing something about it.

This was another trigger point for Michael. He thought, "If they can find creative solutions to a problem, then I can too." The issue that most concerned him at that time was the racism that many immigrants faced when they arrived in the UK. He talked to his friends about what he could do. One pointed out to him, "You can't just go out and do good, you really need to apply some sort of skill or knowledge."

After some thought, Michael decided that the best skill he could use was his ability to speak English, which many immigrants from East Africa and South Asia could not do. In addition to all the discrimination the immigrants experienced in finding housing and employment and the personal abuse that they encountered, they were further isolated by their inability to speak English.

Michael's idea was simple. Volunteers would give an English lesson once a week in the home of an immigrant family. He got addresses of newly arrived families from secondary school head teachers and then knocked on the doors of these families and asked them if they would like a volunteer to come and teach them English.

Almost everyone said "Yes", and the program was soon underway. Within a few months, there were 200 volunteers teaching 200 families in London. And another 70 were helping run what is now known as Supplementary School for Bangladeshi children in East London. This operated five evenings a week, and had arts and sports activities on the weekends.

Michael's project had no name, no money and no bank account. This was before computers and mobile phones, which could have made everything much easier. It was organized from a card index and a landline telephone – a small idea with huge results.

Within a year, the language teaching program started receiving attention and publicity. Head-teachers and directors of education started coming to Michael for advice on what they should be doing about the language problem in their schools. Michael told them, that even though he had no professional expertise in education, English teaching or race policy, he had become The Expert!

This experience made Michael certain about what he wanted to do with his life. After a successful 10-year career in banking and publishing, he decided to use his skills in finance and communication to help change the world. In 1975, he founded the Directory of Social Change, which quickly became the leading provider of information and training to NGOs in the UK, concentrating on fundraising, charity-law, management and communication. This was an early social enterprise, entirely funded from the income it earned. After 20 years; having turned the Directory of Social Change into a multi-million pounds social business, it was time for Michael to move on (for the second time). "Armed with just a desk, a computer and a telephone, I decided to invest my time in creating ideas that would change the world", he says, and that's why he called his new organization – *the Centre for Innovation in Voluntary Action.*

Michael wanted to explore ways in which the ideas and energies of young people could be harnessed to make a difference in the world. In 1994, he co-founded *Changemakers* with three colleagues and became its executive chairperson in order to pioneer the idea of Young Person-Led Community Action.

This bit of jargon sounds a mouthful. But, it essentially means that you don't tell young people what they should do. You first ask them about the issues that concern them, then encourage them to think about what they can do about them, and then finally, support them to go out and do something practical that will make a difference. This can be done either as part of the school curriculum (citizenship education), or in their own time (the lunch hour or after school).

The young people ended up doing everything from building a skateboard park (because that's what they wanted), to setting up an anti-bullying club (a big issue in many schools) or raising money as a memorial to a friend who had died of cancer.

After completing their project, the young people were encouraged to reflect on what they had done (their failures as well as their achievements) and to apply the learning and the new skills that they had developed to their future lives. *Changemakers* remains a successful organization promoting youth leadership through community involvement.

But one thing often leads to another... and then another. *Changemakers* led to *YouthBank UK*, which enabled young people to act as grant-makers, giving away money in their community and for youth projects. They were given complete responsibility for deciding what to support, publicizing their fund, receiving applications, assessing them and making grants, and then ensuring accountability by the people and projects they had supported.

One foundation liked the idea so much that it offered Michael £1,00,000 (around ₹ 1 crore) and this was quickly matched by a second foundation. "I thought it was a great idea, but I did not really know what to do. So, I selected seven youth organizations and offered each of them £25,000 as a grant, on the condition that they worked out for themselves what they intended to do," says Michael.

This provided seven different solutions, and allowed the seven projects to share their different ideas and experiences. Some started with an already formed youth group, others advertised for young people (aged 16 to 25 years) to put themselves forward. Some started with six months of training and some others got going immediately by deciding a grant at their very first meeting.

The idea of *YouthBank* has now spread beyond the UK to Eastern Europe and even Africa. The idea gained momentum and had arrived at its 'tipping point'.

Whilst in India, Michael met a grants officer at the *Ford Foundation*, who offered him $50,000 to establish the idea of *YouthBank* in India, provided that it was run through the National Foundation for India. The money was sufficient to launch four projects in New Delhi – one in a secondary school, one in a college and two with street children.

One of the street children projects turned itself into a Children's Development Bank, where the children could save money (both as a means of keeping any spare cash safe, and also to start saving for their future) and borrow money (to start an income-generating enterprise, as they needed to earn money just to stay alive). Michael then set out to expand the Children's Development Bank across South Asia with the help of New Delhi-based organization *Butterflies* and a grant raised from Comic Relief in the UK.

In 2001, he brought the President of the first bank to a summer camp in the UK, who said, "My dream is that there be a Children's World Bank." That could be a really exciting idea and a challenge for someone to create. Visiting a street children's bank in Dhaka, Michael says, "In Dhaka, I saw a 12-year old in rags opening an account with a crumpled 20 Taka note. This was an extremely moving moment, as I realized that the boy had decided that he will give himself a future, and that that future was worth saving for. This was the first day of his new life!" A little idea had grown into a full-blown movement.

The idea for *MyBnk* partly grew out of this work, as Michael wanted to apply these same ideas in a different context.

Michael subscribes to the philosophy of Lao Tzu, the founder of Taoism, that: "A journey of a thousand miles begins with a single step." He explains it and says, "If you get started, you will eventually get there, though not necessarily where you originally planned. The journey may not be smooth, but zig-zag; with persistence and energy you will get there. But, if you fail to take that all-important first step, you get nowhere. Things will just stay as they are."

It does not end here... There are many other ideas that Michael has worked on or helped others to develop during the past few years.

One such idea is called *Otesha*. The premise is that we need to live more sustainably with the world providing opportunities for more people. Young people can take this message out to other young people through cycle tours and staging plays and discussions. Young people walk the talk or rather cycle it, unlike pompous politicians who keep telling others what's the right thing to do. Managing the food cycle is another of his ideas. Everyone knows that a lot of food is wasted in an increasingly hungry world and that we need to do something about it. Michael helped students and community groups find food that was otherwise thrown away by markets and supermarkets, cook it in a donated kitchen space and then serve it to hungry people such as the homeless, refugees and the old. The latest idea is a chain of community restaurants that use reclaimed food which is called *Pie in the Sky*. This teaches young people about cooking and healthy eating, as well as providing a creative use for food that is otherwise wasted or thrown away.

Another project called Farm shop encourages the creation of a farm inside a shop, so as to promote local farmers and their produce. Property owners are starting to get interested.

In 2000, Michael formed a consortium to bid for a £100 million fund provided by the UK National Lottery to be used as an endowment (corpus) for a grants fund, whose aim would be to benefit individuals in the UK. The consortium consisted of organizations, which were promoting social entrepreneurship. They won the bid against stiff competition. This was how UnLtd was created to 'Invest in Individuals with Ideas' – these are the three Is of social change.

UnLtd has been very successful. Michael is helping spread it to other countries, including South Africa, China and Hong Kong. UnLtd India started in Mumbai in 2007, and has supported the development of projects such as: Reality Tours (tourist trips to Dharavi slum, where 80 percent of profits go towards supporting a youth center), Under the Mango Tree (promoting bee-keeping as a livelihood and increasing pollination by training bee-keepers and selling honey) and Oscar (encouraging underprivileged children to play football and also promoting literacy among them).

In 2005, Michael wrote a book titled *365 Ways to Change the World*, which has been published around the world, first in the UK (in three editions) and then in ten other countries including India, China, USA, Australia and South Africa, each edition particularly relevant to the country of publication.

When asked about the inspiration behind the book, he said, "There are lots of issues in the world that need to be addressed, from corruption to hunger and from disease to apathy. If you look at a big issue each day and can do something small to address that issue, you will learn that you really can make a difference. Even if it's something quite small, lots of people doing something will make a huge difference. And doing something small can also encourage you to go on and do bigger and better things."

As he approaches his 70th birthday, Michael is busier than ever. The ideas keep on coming...

He has been appointed as the professor of social entrepreneurship at the University of Cape Town in South Africa to help them establish a Centre for Social Innovation and Entrepreneurship. He is also mentoring around 20 social entrepreneurs working on ideas that range from setting up a fish-farm inside containers and creating an enterprise by putting on music gigs, to pop-up youth clubs and one-to-one literacy teaching in unusual environments.

He has also just taken on the role of a philanthropy instructor at Beijing Normal University, which will enable him to spread his ideas even more widely.

Michael sums up his philosophy as follows:

"It is ideas that change the world. We humans are blessed with brains, and we should use these to devise solutions to the world's big problems, as well as to the smaller problems in the communities and society around us.

"The biggest problem in the world is not poverty, disease, hunger, corruption... It is apathy – the fact that we can see the problems, but either ignore them or are too lazy to do anything about them. If nobody does anything, nothing will happen. If one person takes that first step, then anything becomes possible. I really believe that trying is more important than succeeding!"

As the Irish playwright Samuel Beckett says, "No matter, fail again. Next time, fail better". This is Michael's philosophy, and he urges anyone who sees a problem to come up with their own solution and give it a go.

BIOGRAPHER

Lily Lapenna is the CEO and founder of UK-based social enterprise MyBnk.

Together with the MyBnk team, Lily has created a series of learning programs that range from money management workshops to the first independent youth led online and in-school banking scheme.

In the last six years, Lily has taken MyBnk from a single pilot project to an organization reaching over 60,000 young people.

What the world needs is not simply charity, but inclusive social justice. The idea of Joy of Giving is to try and encourage a grassroots change in the mindset to stimulate a win-win framework of thought, with fairness and equality for all.

– Jeroninio

The Audacity of Dreams

Vijay Mehta

From a tiny inch-sized acorn, to a towering giant oak
From a speck, to an invaluable pearl of enduring beauty
From a vision and an ardent dream
To international organizations of great magnitude...

The litmus test of a true enterprise revolves around how much it can contribute towards development and to laying strong foundations, where growth begets growth and quality begets quality. It is with this belief that *Uniting for Peace* has embarked on its chosen mission. This ardent belief inspires it to strive harder and look beyond the milestones of achievement.

If we cannot envision the world we want to live in, we cannot work towards its creation. If we cannot place ourselves in our imagination, it is hard to believe it is possible. When people can see a vision and simultaneously recognize what can be done taking one step at a time with dedication and sincerity to achieve it, they will begin to feel encouragement and enthusiasm instead of fright. The entry into the new millennium demands implementation of a positive vision for the future – one which draws closer people and nations.

One such great visionary is Vijay Mehta.

Vijay was born on April 9, 1940 in New Delhi. As a young boy, he used to accompany his father, KL Mehta, a liberal solicitor in pre-independent India, to prayer meetings convened by the 'Great Light' – Mohandas Karamchand Gandhi. His father used to narrate stories about legendary leaders of the time, especially Gandhiji, who became a great source of inspiration and whose influence greatly molded his mind. Gandhiji's message of non-violence struck a chord in young Vijay's mind – a chord that resonated throughout his life to shape his character and life's mission, and his thoughts about the world and humanity as a whole. The thoughts of other great men, many writings and many books have also enriched his mind.

Not only his father, but his grandfather Lala TD Mehta, who had been a distinguished social reformer and champion of Hindu-Muslim unity, was an inspiration too. His august personality towered over all family members. He taught Vijay to develop a world vision. At that time, people thought of themselves as either Hindus or Muslims, and this prompted separatism. This, he believes, greatly harms the growth of the nation. Setting aside casteism, he wanted all of them to be Indians first. The spirit of secularism propagated by him was an eye-opener and came to be accepted as a positive approach to world peace.

How lucky he was to have a father and grandfather with such noble and beautiful thoughts! He was interested in everything and delighted in sharing their enthusiasm. As a child, he was full of questions, and this enabled them to tell him about the world, about the men and women who inhabited it and who moved others by their ideas and actions. Above all, they loved to speak about the country and its early achievements. Growing up with their teachings, companionship and guidance, inspired Vijay to be ever enthusiastic.

Having graduated from Hindu College, New Delhi he went on to complete his masters at the University of

Delhi, the city in which he met his wife Shanti. In the late 1960s, Vijay moved to England to pursue a new life and they welcomed into the world four children – Sanjay, Vimal, Ajay and Renu. He ventured into the clothing industry with remarkable success, but found himself moving towards a totally different enterprise which was fuelled by his dreams. By the 1980s, the well-established business was handed over to the next generation.

When one acts according to one's loftiest dreams, the outcome is often far grander than one can imagine. His true vocation took roots as the co-founder and chair of Uniting for Peace, a responsibility which he still holds. He is the president of Mehta Centre and the founding trustee of Fortune Forum Charity. He is a renowned author, a champion of truth and a global activist for peace, development, human rights and environment. Vijay found himself going far beyond his first vision to a much greater passion and enterprise by choosing a path, which was his mission and purpose.

Vijay has a strict work ethic. He comes to office every day to write, prepares for talks and strategizes how best to spread the words of peace. He enjoys long walks, yoga and meditation. He is a vegetarian and teetotaler and has herbal tea based on his own recipe. He loves reading books and newspapers.

Today, as a renowned activist for peace, development and human rights, he works tirelessly around the world to help sow the seeds which will bring an end to wars, militarism and poverty. The vision of an ideal and deep dedication to the cause gives him the strength to carry on. Vijay is intensely involved, unbending, lofty, cool and fearless, qualities that make him a unique leader and a great peace-activist who looks at the world as indivisible.

The *Bhagavad Gita* states, "The actions of a great man are an inspiration for others. Whatever he does becomes a standard for others to follow." It indeed stands true for Vijay.

He is the co-founder and chairperson of *Uniting for Peace*, which is devoted to building and promoting a global culture of peace, non-violence and poverty-alienation, one of whose creators was Philip Noel Baker, a recipient of the Nobel Peace Prize (1959). Efforts to promote universal peace, non-violence and poverty-alleviation have been given a thrust since 1979. The institution is striving continuously to avert the prospect of nuclear annihilation. Vijay's second career as a votary of peace led him around the world, from Belfast to The Hague and back to his homeland, India, a country still rocked by unseen conflicts so often ignored by those who focus on the metro cities, highways and Bollywood glamour.

The entry into the new millennium provides an ideal opportunity to pledge and implement a positive vision for the future – to bring together all countries towards a common goal. Harnessing current trends, executing future focused projects, garnering powerful resources, working closely, productively, effectively and qualitatively is the true vision. The true karma of a leader is humanity at heart. For an enterprise to ally itself with a great purpose, it must have courage, conviction, discipline and endurance – qualities which engender organizational growth and all-round success.

Vijay's untiring efforts in this direction go on to promote the United Nations Millennium Development Goals by 2015. As a founding trustee of Fortune Forum Charity, he along with his daughter Renu Mehta, the founder of Fortune Forum Charity, held three summits in London in 2006, 2007 and 2008. The summits attracted a worldwide audience of 1.3 billion people (one-fifth of humanity) including print and media people. The keynote speakers for the first and second summit were Bill Clinton, former US President and Al Gore, former US Vice-President, and the recipient of the Nobel Peace Prize 2007. Vijay addressed and attended many international conferences and served on many advisory boards and forums to address the dynamics between peace and disarmament, offering dialogue and non-violent solutions to tackle conflict.

His actions show that every successful human endeavor is a consequence of the right combination of elements – a fiery determination, focused direction and forceful impetus. These are the elements that spark off and sustain the saga of progress. These are the forces of human nature which when combined with the vision, create and conceive new worlds of achievement, transforming ideas into reality.

Through his peace missions, Vijay came across many influential luminaries, including Nobel Peace Prize winners Mairead Maguire, Dr Shirin Ebaadi and Archbishop Desmond Tutu. He galvanizes everyone he meets with his boundless energy, optimism and passion to effect change amid the chaos, violence and unpredictability in society. As the chairperson and activist of Uniting for Peace Mission campaigning has provided an opportunity for extensive travel around the globe advocating peace, ending arms trade and militarism, poverty reduction and sustainable development.

Thank you for all you do, Vijay – both the organization and you, are an inspiration and give us hope that Uniting for Peace can bring a world without war. Indeed, it is possible, even in our own time.

– Mairead Corrigan Maguire
(United Kingdom/Northern Ireland),
Nobel Peace Laureate (1976)

BIOGRAPHER

Jyothi Gosala is the agency chief of Shubang Communications, publisher and editor of Conversations and a professional compère in English. She was the advisory member of the *Discovery* Magazine and Loksatta Party. She was a compère in English for All India Radio, Hyderabad. Jyothi holds master's degrees in communication and journalism (Osmania University) and has done an M.Sc in psychology (University of Madras). She is a graduate of the Indian Business School in entrepreneurship. She is also a black belt holder in karate.

We are all ordinary people; mere mortals who will turn into ashes and dust one day. There is however, power and greatness within us that can be unleashed in the service of society to make us extraordinary, limitless and immortal. The day we realize this, our life will be filled with meaning and purpose.

– Jeroninio

Let's Go Help Somebody

Arzell Paparazell

"Let's go help somebody." This phrase was uttered simply and naively by one boy to another, a very long time ago, as if helping others was no different than tying one's shoe laces at the beginning of the day. 'Let's go help somebody' represented the first step on a journey of ten million steps, which this boy – Arzell Paparazell Nelson – began a lifetime ago, and which continues even today.

Arzell was greatly influenced by his parents, Willie and Parrie, and also his grandparents, Nettie and George Johnson. They were music connoisseurs. His father played the saxophone and his mother the piano. She also sang Gospel music. Arzell's grandmother played blues guitar and sang the blues. His elder brothers were rock-and-roll musicians and singers.

As has often been demonstrated, the genesis of a compassionate and caring heart lies in some childhood influence. Arzell's need to help others was shaped from his personal need for help. After his third birthday, Arzell could not speak for almost two years. Something went wrong with his vocal cords and he could not make any sound. The doctors said that only surgery could fix the problem. Undeterred by the dire prognosis, Arzell's father gave him a homemade flute and taught him to communicate with everyone through music.

The homemade flute became his voice. Soon, he started playing other musical instruments. He learned to communicate and express himself through music. He never missed a beat. In spite of his medical condition, Arzell never missed out on school or life in general. Thanks to his father, what could have been a catastrophic period of silence for a small boy became a time of beautiful sounds and growth. Arzell understood that the sound from his flute, like the many voices in the world, is ultimately an instrument of universal communication.

'Let's go help somebody,' was the launch-pad through which Arzell turned his attentions away from his own problems and toward others. His only working plan was cosmic in nature, invisibly guiding a young man on his quest to make the world a better place. As he found his path, his vocal cords healed and his voice returned. Simply put, it meant doing whatever was necessary to help out. Sometimes that involved taking up a job, any job. At other times, it meant working as a volunteer, without pay, or knocking on doors asking for help or offering help. The means of helping others didn't matter. The ends – to help the needy – always mattered.

For Arzell, it all began in Over the Rhine, a neighborhood in his hometown Cincinnati, Ohio. It was there that he followed his calling to help, using music as his main tool of communication, along with his ability to be compassionate, which he learned from his parents.

The lesson Arzell learned from his father was on full display as he realized that the best way to help people was through music and human relations. In fact, if you ask others to describe him, they would tell you three things: he is a musician, he helps others and he knows a lot of people who can get things done. He has molded himself to become a human connection between those who need and those who have.

"I was very young when I realized that music could be used to bring attention to human rights issues, poverty and human suffering... I used music to deal with juvenile delinquency, racism, sexism and cultural and social isolation," he says.

His music and people-skills have taken him around the world, enabling him to work with people from different continents, while maintaining his roots in his hometown. Arzell has garnered universal and award-winning praise for jazz piano and for musical compositions including his musical 'Little Boy Jazz' performed at the Tony award-winning 'Playhouse in the Park Marx Theatre'. As a composer, he has written five musicals and over 300 songs. His earlier compositions were recorded during the mid-1970s in New York City at Columbia Records. His music, at that time, bore contemporary style and most of his musical arrangements were of the disco/dance genres. Arzell has opened up for artists Stanley Turentine, Jeff Lober, Hiroshima, Phylis Hyman (in the 1980s, he produced a concert video of Ms Hyman), Philip Bailey, George Dukes, Freddie Hubbard and David Valentine (flute). During the 1980s and the 1990s, Arzell promoted concerts of Prince (Purple Haze Concert), Freddie Jackson, Melba Moore, Whispers, Barry White, Huey Lewis and The News, Destiny's child, Jagged Edge, John B, De Barge, Stevie Wonder, Gil Scott Heron, Richie Havens, besides the 'Coors and Budweiser Jazz Explosion Concert Series'.

Although well-traveled, Arzell remains connected to his roots. For a long time, he worked for the Cincinnati Human Relations Commission and retired as its executive director in 1998. During his tenure, Arzell was presented the key to the City of Cincinnati by three mayors. Former Ohio Governor George Voinovich, recognized his work with proclamations on two occasions for civic leadership and for promoting cultural diversity. President Bill Clinton recognized Arzell with two letters of appreciation for services rendered. Among many awards, he has been conferred the Berry-Gottschalk Award (named after two great civic leaders, Theodore M. Berry and Rabbi Alfred Gottschalk) by The Race Relations Council of Greater Cincinnati for providing local, regional and national training programs for the police departments and community relations departments.

Arzell developed community concerts and art performances to raise money for other projects such as the Free Store Food Bank, of which he is a founding member. He later went on to oversee the "share food" program, which provided supplemental food to poor, middle-class and non-means tested citizens from five cities in the United States.

Arzell believes that it is unfortunate that many of us would choose not to forgive but would rather choose a path of conflict and confrontation. Such people find ways to justify their aggressive behaviour by filling their mind, soul and body with negativity and by thinking up 'excuses' as to why we cannot forge ahead with positive activity.

Today, Arzell is the chief executive officer of L'lezra Entertainment Group that creates music and documentaries. He runs the company with his long-time associate, Abraham Cheatham, and his wife, Cynthia Lockett-Nelson, who is its chief operating officer. Over 30 artists have signed up with the company and their music ranges from hip-hop, jazz, rock/blues, reggae, pop, trance, dance, world beat and r and b/soul. These artists conduct concerts and programs, the proceeds of which are utilized for those in need.

Arzell is currently working on a documentary titled, *Don't count me out*, which focuses on problems that women, children and minority populations face on a daily basis. The stories in the documentary have been taken from around the world. The documentary highlights the ways and means that citizens, both individuals and groups, have developed as lasting solutions to these many problems. Arzell puts it simply, "We choose individual moments of grandeur over the collective acts of humanity. Thus, the work of building a strong foundation is at a constant risk of not being built properly."

When not making or producing documentaries and musical compositions, Arzell provides training to both public and private corporations and organizations in the USA and the world on how to cope with and solve human relations issues, desegregation, diversity training, and also crisis-intervention for various police and fire departments.

In 2012, following his return from India, Arzell had a major surgery to repair an abdominal aortic aneurysm rupture – a near-death experience to which he responds, "I am always within and never without." He adds, "I remember being lonely as a child, because of my inability to talk, but my dad's response saved me because he gave me compassionate attention. Today, I'm alive because of 'compassion'. I emphasize that what the world needs now is more compassion."

A champion of human rights, Arzell believes, "Having a house is important. A house is symbolic of growth. We do not build enough number of houses, hence young people remain homeless. We are also the 'housekeepers' of the world. When will we build our own 'house' (house of unity and compassion)? We must build a house of love for each other, a house of economic prosperity for each other, a house of cultural and historical education for each other and a house in which we all can feel safe and protected." He feels that efforts to foster and promote goodwill are often abandoned because of egos, greed, arrogance and ignorance. "We should try to come together to create something bigger than ourselves and create a sense within ourselves that there is a 'higher calling' which we recognize as divine love, wisdom, power, joy, peace, compassion, grace and truth," he says.

Arzell, in one of his speeches, said, "We lose time because we choose to spend our time challenging each other with personal and professional debates that have nothing to do with our humanitarian cause. We create an unnecessary battleground of egos, being at each other's throats and smacking the face of human dignity without any remorse. Only our egos and selfishness can lead us to abandon our principles of kindness, civility and forgiveness. We spend hours trying to prove to one another, who is right or wrong, when at the end of the day, the problems of hunger, homelessness, joblessness and blatant crimes against humanity continue to occur."

BIOGRAPHER

Jo Anne Moore is a writer living and working in her hometown of Cincinnati, Ohio. A former broadcast journalist, Moore is also the owner and author of *The Skeptik One* Blog, a published work of short stories, as well as political and topical articles filled with observations about surrounding life.

Humans are rational animals and have the power to think and choose. Our personalities are therefore not limited or constrained by nature and nurture. Thus, we need not be the victims of our situation. We have the power to become whatever we choose.

– Jeroninio

His Pictures are Worth a Thousand Deeds

Mahesh Bhat

"Frankly, if you ask me why I decided to create UNSUNG, I would say that I was destined to do it," says Mahesh Bhat, the book's photographer and publisher. UNSUNG is a project about true heroes – people who have contributed to society against great personal odds.

It all began in 1986, when Mahesh boarded a train to New Delhi. He was still a BSc, student in Mangalore and did not have the slightest idea that this journey would mark the genesis of his book. Mahesh was on his way to meet senior photojournalists TS Satyan, Raghu Rai and a few others, to seek advice about pursuing a career in photography. "I was, in fact, thinking of dropping out of college to pursue a full-time career in photography. Satyan asked me to tread carefully on this career path. Raghu, un-fortunately, was away shooting in Kolkata. So, Satyan told me to meet S. Paul, Raghu's brother and mentor. When I trekked across to Paul's house one morning, he was about to leave for Bharatapur to cover a forest-fire there. Yet, he took time out for me, went through my pictures and interacted with me. He was the one who wholeheartedly endorsed my idea of dropping out of college to pursue photography," says Mahesh.

The visit to New Delhi had indeed shown him a new path. Mahesh came back to Mangalore, quit college and moved to Bengaluru in search of work as a photographer. In the initial stages, he worked as an assistant to advertising photographer Kiran Kumar. In 1988, he was offered the opportunity to work on a book on Karnataka. From 1989 onwards, he worked as an advertising and editorial photographer in Bengaluru. He was a photographer for many top advertising agencies and periodicals. He also published a magazine called *Light*, which was devoted to visual thinking. It was the first of its kind in India. In 1995, Mahesh founded a multimedia design and visual web design company. Unfortunately, in spite of doing pioneering work, it didn't do well financially and was closed down. Although Mahesh would keep very busy, that episode on the train from Mangalore to New Delhi remained with him. Sometime in 2002, he remembered that incident again during another train journey.

This journey was of three nights and four days. The train had just arrived at the Nagpur station on the second evening of the journey. In those days, the train would go down to Palghat, Kerala, turn around at the Palghat Gap and then make a long run to New Delhi. The next morning, it would stop in Bhopal. Mahesh remembers that a poor lady with a baby boarded the train at Nagpur and sat near the entrance of the coach. Some passengers in Mahesh's compartment asked her to leave, as she did not have a res- ervation. However, Mahesh and some others thought that she could stay, since she was going to get off at Bhopal the next morning itself. And so, she stayed.

Meanwhile, this lady who was seated opposite Mahesh, started narrating her story. She revealed that she was trying to reach Bhopal as early as possible. She had lost her mother to the Bhopal gas tragedy and a telegram that afternoon had conveyed that her father's condition was critical. However, her husband, an auto mechanic, had forbidden her to go. Yet, she had fought with him and rushed to the railway station. After the tragedy, she and her family were promised a compensation of ₹ 10,000, but they had received only ₹ 5,000. She said that a clerk at the government office had pocketed the remaining amount.

The lady's story and her plight left an indelible impression on Mahesh's mind. In a way, it set the base for UNSUNG; his concept of 'Photography for Change' developed out of this very interaction. In those days, whether it was in the advertising industry or in mainstream magazines, using photography to bring about change was unheard of.

For Mahesh, it was through photography that he could give back to society and make a difference in people's lives. Just as he had decided to make a career in photography, his urge to bring about such change was born out of his passion for it. And that's how UNSUNG began.

So, what is UNSUNG all about?

Mahesh's basic idea was to build a platform to discuss and create awareness about changemakers. When one hears about this objective, one is prompted to ask the question 'why'. With a fulfilling career in photography, it seemed imperative for Mahesh to have a larger motivation to undertake a project like UNSUNG.

There are enough reasons not to start a project like this. For one, there is not enough money. Based on the advice of Jayapriya Vasudevan, a literary agent, Mahesh spoke to corporates in the hope of garnering some financial support for the project. Infosys, Ganjam and HCL supported the project by under writing certain number of copies and advancing the money to do the project. When he approached Anita Pratap to write for the book, she readily agreed. It took over four years to raise the funds and slowly chip away at it. Mahindra, Vodafone, CNN-IBN and Brigade Group stepped in later on with their support. Finally, the book was ready for publication in 2007. With 3,000 copies pre-sold, there was enough money to print 6,500 copies. So, in September 2007, *UNSUNG* hit the shelves.

Over the last five years, *UNSUNG* has made a great amount of positive contribution to the lives of the 'heroes' featured in it. Help poured in for the projects these heroes have been pursuing, and in turn, the heroes have been able to help thousands in need. Till date, with the help of awareness created by *UNSUNG,* over ₹ 90 lakh have been raised towards the different causes featured in it. Stories from the book were used as case studies at the Indian Institute of Management-Bangalore (IIM-B). Several heroes have been invited by the IIM-B to visit the campus and address the students.

Mahesh has traveled around speaking about *UNSUNG* to small informal groups of people as well as large formal gatherings. He was asked the same question by many – "Neither do I have the ability to be a changemaker like the people that are featured in your book, nor do I have that much money to donate…is there something that I can learn from all of them and adapt?" This led him to reflect upon the book and he realized that all the nine heroes in the book had one common trait that made them who they were. "I realized that in every *UNSUNG* hero, there was a complete alignment of thought, word and deed," he says. He later realized that these were the first three steps in the eight-fold path described by Buddha. He says that most of our problems rise from the fact that our thoughts, words and deeds are totally at disarray. To maintain this alignment is not easy, says Mahesh, because it needs a lot of courage. "I am trying to adapt this philosophy into my life, but I haven't yet succeeded completely," he adds.

UNSUNG has inspired philanthropic individuals to fund the next book, which will feature the stories of another nine extraordinary individuals. Six other photographers have collaborated and the content for the next book is almost ready. MindTree has also come forward to make a downloadable app for iPad and Android tablets as a pro bono service. Today, *UNSUNG* has an interactive website that spreads the stories further. In Mahesh's words, it has and continues to be a fulfilling experience.

But why did he decide to do it? "Photojournalism is a very interesting profession. It lets you travel, take a peek into the lives of diverse people and explore the entire spectrum of life. In the mid-nineties, during the course of my work, I began meeting people, who were making a difference against great personal odds. On the other hand, most young people were growing up under the influence of what television channels were dishing out. Their role models were movie stars, cricketers and fashion models. Indians really did not have heroes – people who they could look up to and emulate. But, I discovered heroes right there among us. They were working with the singular focus of positively changing society. While we partied, they were holding our social fabric together. The idea of this book, germinated then," says Mahesh in his introduction to the book. He believes that there are not enough positive stories on the Internet, or the television, or the newspapers as there should be. His destiny led him to the book and he says that it has even led to some personal transformations.

As he speaks of such realizations and treasures many other manifestations, Mahesh strives to find ways in which he can induce change through his photography. In what seems like destiny's first insight, *UNSUNG* is just one among what his destiny has in store for him.

Mahesh lives on the outskirts of Bengaluru with his wife, Odissi dancer Bijayini Satpathy, on their organic farm.

The place was a patch of barren land when they bought it around 11 years ago. Today, it has transformed into a beautiful farm with lots of trees. He is actively involved in preserving the local eco-system and is currently engaged in getting a 300-acre grassland adjoining his farm declared a protected zone. He has recently released a book called *Bengaluru/Bangalore – In First Person Singular,* which is an impassioned plea to support art and creativity to drive the true growth of the city. There are three more books and a feature film project in the pipeline.

Mahesh is the co-founder and head of photography school of The One School Goa, an interdisciplinary creative media school, located in Uccasaim Goa. Mahesh photographs for publications and corporations from across the world. He has been commissioned by clients from over 20 countries around the world. He is also on the board of advisors and a visiting faculty at the Symbiosis School of Photography in Pune.

BIOGRAPHER

Archana Nathan is a young writer based in Bengaluru. She studied at St. Xavier's College in Mumbai and has briefly worked for *The New Indian Express.*

The value of our life can be measured by the number of times we have been so deeply stirred that we had to stand up, speak out and remove the misery of the world around us.

– Jeroninio

Where There's a Will, There's Definitely a Way

Mark Parkinson

"There won't be a job for you this year. Lots of people are out of work. Never mind, I'm sure you'll find something to do with your summer vacation!" My heart lurched as I heard these words from my mother in the car on the way home from boarding school for the summer vacation.

I was 15 then and just the year before, I had had the time of my life when I spent my summer vacation working on a farm. At 15, the economy doesn't mean too much to you, but I was aware of the economic downturn through newspapers running front-page news about recession, unemployment and hard times. However, until this moment I hadn't given any thought to the idea that it might mean something to me. This was a shocker.

For weeks I had been remembering the thrill of being useful and productive alongside adults. I loved the feedback that came to me at the end of every week of my pay packet as evidence that I had contributed and given something of value. I loved the sense of satisfaction that came from not needing pocket money from my parents, so they could do other things with the money. I loved the planning for how I would spend my hard-earned pay. So, to my young mind it was very simple – I would pay no heed to my mother's warning.

The next day, after an early breakfast, I headed out to visit all the most common places where young students got summer jobs: shops, hotels, restaurants, city offices… I carried some sandwiches so that I wouldn't need to go home for lunch. I sat down to eat them outside the busy job centre. Moments before, a nice lady had shaken her head at me and told me the same thing my mother had told me the day before.

By 5:30 that evening, my feet were hurting, my back was aching and I was tired and hungry. Nothing positive had materialized, so I headed home. My mother was as sympathetic as she could be, but I think she sensed that it wasn't sympathy I wanted.

The next morning, I repeated the exercise – covering a different part of town. I knocked on doors, spent time waiting in offices, only to be told over and over, "Sorry, we don't have anything this year." Today, I headed home for lunch. As I finished eating, my mother enquired how I planned to spend my time, "seeing as you don't have a job this year." I looked her in the eye and responded with absolute confidence, "Yet."

"But, you've tried everywhere," she replied. I understood that like any protective parent she wanted to protect me from hurt feelings.

"There's one place I haven't been to yet: the industrial estate. I'm going there this afternoon," I said.

"Okay," she replied, adding, "but I can't believe the companies there will have anything for someone your age."

After I'd finished lunch, I wheeled out my bike and headed off on the four-mile journey to the industrial estate. There were around 100 companies of varying sizes spread around a broad arc with various side-offshoots. My plan was a simple one. Start at one end and visit every place until I got to the other end. After the first 10, any passive observer would have considered my mother's prediction to be correct. At some places, I was treated dismissively, looked up and down and even laughed at. At about the 15th place, I was asked whether I could use a screw driver and paint.

A middle-aged man showed me into a room, where he explained that there was about a week's work available. This involved putting some metal shelves together and painting them. I looked him in the eye and said, "I'll get back to you for this work only if I don't get something for the whole nine weeks of the summer. That's what I'm really looking for."

With a quick handshake and a smile, I was back on the road. The afternoon wore on as I systematically approached every single building on the estate. Shortly before 5 pm. I walked up a short path to the last place on the whole estate. It was a company dealing with lawn mowers. There was a showroom with everything from little push mowers for the garden to large industrial mowers for golf courses and race-courses. As I walked through the door, I could see a spare parts department to my right and a sign leading to an area further back marked 'workshop' for servicing and repairs. In the middle of the showroom, stood two businessmen in suits.

I walked up to them, waited as they ended their conversation and turned to find out what I wanted and boldly stated, "I'm here for a summer job. I'm available for nine weeks. I'm a hard worker." The man on the left, who turned out to be the managing director, looked at this skinny, lanky 15-year-old, smiled and asked, "Can you do filing?"

Well, as someone who kept his books and music collections in alphabetic order (yes, some people might find that funny), I felt completely confident to answer in the affirmative.

"Well, you're in luck, young man. We just sacked the filing clerk about 15 minutes ago. We should have done it ages ago. The filing system is in a complete mess. If you think you're up to it, you can start at 9 am tomorrow," he said.

"I'll be here," I assured him. The briefest of discussions about money followed, though quite frankly, I would have accepted pretty much whatever was offered. Both men put out their hands to shake mine. As I headed out of the door, I almost shook with thrill and excitement. The smile remained fixed on my face for days.

At 8:50 am the next day, I reported for work – dressed as the smartest 15-year-old for miles around. I worked through the whole summer, loving that job like I've probably never loved any other. In the nine weeks that followed, I sorted out the problems with the filing system to the point of zero-filing errors or zero-missed files and for good measure I redesigned the billing for mower repairs, therefore saving the company a lot of money.

To think, today, many would call that child labour, but I wouldn't have let anyone take that opportunity away from me for anything.

WRITER

Until 1996, **Mark Parkinson** was a successful private banking manager in the UK. However, when he realized success didn't necessarily bring fulfillment, he set about reinventing himself as an educator. From 2007 to 2012, he was the director of the reputed The Shri Ram Schools in New Delhi and Gurgaon, leading them to number one day school rank in 2008, 2009 and 2011. A passionate sports lover, he supports the development of grassroots rugby in India.

Our children and youth need to be encouraged to become voices of conscience and voices of dissent. We must encourage them to ask questions, to stand up and speak out for what they believe and to challenge dogma.

– Jeroninio

A Will Will Find its Way

Subhasini Mistry

Misfortune dogged Subhasini Mistry from the moment of her birth. She was born during the Bengal famine that drove impoverished farmers to starvation and death across the countryside. Her father, a marginal farmer who owned a tiny patch of land in Kulwa village about 30 kilometers south west of Kolkata, was unable to feed his 14 children. Her mother scoured the land, begging for rice from the churches, *ashrams*, NGOs, government offices and landlords of the area. Over the next few years, seven of the children died.

At 12, Subhasini was married off to Chandra, an agricultural worker who lived in Hanspukur village, a one-and-a-half hour walk away. He earned ₹ 200 a month. Subhasini struggled to make ends meet, cooking and cleaning all day for her husband and four children.

Disaster struck in 1971. Her husband began writhing in pain and she rushed him to the district hospital in Tollygunge, Kolkata. The anxiety over her husband's deteriorating condition gave way to horror as she realized that the doctors and nurses refused to pay any attention to him because he was penniless. This government hospital was mandated to provide free service to the poor. But, reality was that patients needed either money or connections to get treatment. Death ended her husband's torment.

But, that was only the beginning of Subhasini's torment. Her husband was the sole breadwinner of the family. She was poor and illiterate with four small frightened and hungry children to raise. She sobbed over the body of her dead husband, overcome with grief and desperation. A poor, puny housewife with no education, training or skills, how on earth was she going to raise her four children, the eldest eight-years-old, the youngest not even two? Her parents and brothers were so poor, they could barely support themselves.

Through her tears and fears, Subhasini made an oath that fateful day. No one should suffer her fate. Basic medical attention could easily have saved her husband who had nothing more than a bout of gastroenteritis. But, poverty and callous hospital staff had killed her husband. She vowed she would do what it takes to spare people of this nightmare. She would build a hospital for the poor.

But, Subhasini did not have the luxury to indulge in either her dream or her despair. She had four hungry mouths to feed. She only knew housework, so she started working as a maid servant in five houses nearby, earning a total of ₹ 100 a month. She recalls, "There is no work my hands have not done. I have cooked, mopped floors, washed utensils, cleaned gardens, polished shoes and concreted roofs." Her son Ajoy was a good student. She sent him to an orphanage in Kolkata so he could get a decent education. The other three children helped with housework.

Soon, she discovered she could pick vegetables that grew on the wayside in Dhapa village and sell them. She realized that selling vegetables would fetch more money than doing other people's housework. So, she and her children moved to Dhapa village where she rented a hut for ₹ 5 a month. She began selling vegetables in Dhapa village, and gradually, as her business grew, she headed for bustling Kolkata. She set up her wayside stall on bridge number four in Park Circus in central Kolkata. She started earning about ₹ 500 a month. During the cauliflower season, she earned more. She opened a savings account in the post office and deposited a little money whenever she could. Sometimes ₹ 50, sometimes ₹ 200.

For 20 years, she scrimped and saved. She spent nothing on herself and little on her children, except for Ajoy's education. With the industriousness of an ant, she saved, little by little. For a purpose. She had not given up on her dream. She was determined to build that hospital.

In 1992, she bought one acre of land in her husband's village, Hanspukur, for ₹ 10,000. She moved back with her children to her husband's hut that had been lying vacant all along nearby. She gathered the villagers and told them of her plan. She would donate her one acre land for the hospital, but the villagers would have to donate money to build a thatched shed that could serve as a dispensary for the poor. The public donation totaled to ₹ 926. Some villagers contributed in kind – providing bamboos, palm leaves, truckloads of earth and wooden planks. The poorest offered their labor. Thus, a 20 feet by 20 feet temporary shed was constructed in 1993. Then, an auto rickshaw fitted with a loudspeaker plied the countryside over a 10 kilometer radius, pleading with doctors to offer their free service at the newly opened Hanspukur shed at least once a week for the poor and the needy. Simultaneously, villagers went from door to door urging residents to donate their surplus medicines.

The first doctor to respond to the call was Dr Raghupathy Chatterjee. Five others followed in rapid succession – a general physician, pediatrician, orthopedic, ophthalmologist and a homeopath. Each one of them offered free service, ranging from two to four hours a week. On the very first day,

252 patients were treated. Humanity Hospital, as the little shed was named, never looked back.

Not that the going was easy. Monsoon was pure hell. There was knee-deep water inside the shed. The patients had to be treated on the road. So, it was decided to build a concrete roof covering a 1,000 sq feet area. This required much more money. So, Subhasini and her son Ajoy cast the net wider.

Ajoy knocked on the door of the local Member of Parliament, Malini Bhattacharya. At first, he made no headway. The door remained firmly shut. But, he persisted. Bit by bit, the door opened and finally he managed to meet the MP and explained his mother's goal. Over a period of time, he won her over and after seeing with her own eyes Subhasini's single-minded devotion to her charitable work, Malini supported the Humanity Hospital wholeheartedly. She helped them to raise sufficient funds and so the foundation stone was laid in 1993. Not a single reporter attended the event. However, after the hospital was constructed, with Malini's and the local MLA's help, Subhasini was able to get the governor of West Bengal to inaugurate it. The governor's presence ensured the presence of a flock of reporters. The media coverage had a healthy fall out – a trickle, though not a torrent, of donations followed.

In the meantime, Ajoy got admitted into the prestigious Kolkaka Medical College and after graduation, attended to the day-to-day running of the Humanity Hospital. A group of trustees – including doctors, eminent local citizens and serving IPS officers – guided the hospital, which has now expanded to include gynecology, cardiology, ENT, urology, oncology, diabetology and surgery. They now have three acres of land and the hospital has expanded to 9,000 sq feet, spread over two floors.

Through all this growth, Subhasini was clear about her goal. This was a hospital for the poor. This was not a business. Yet, she knew that the hospital had to be self-sufficient. It cannot survive forever on donations. So, while the poor got free treatment, those who lived above poverty line had to pay ₹ 10 for consultation. Still, this was not sufficient to cover the day-to-day expense of running a hospital. "There is a perpetual shortage of funds. We live from month to month," reveals Ajoy.

How did she achieve all this? She says: "Inner strength." She adds with rustic wisdom, "God in his infinite grace gave me a vision at the darkest moment in my life. From then on, my life had a purpose. I used whatever strength God gave me to make sure other poor people did not lose their loved ones for lack of medical attention."

With her son Ajoy at the helm of the hospital, the doughty Subhasini went back to doing what she knew best – selling vegetables, back at bridge number four. She still lives in the same house. Her elder daughter and son too sell vegetables. Her youngest daughter has become a nurse and works in the hospital.

If she had kept all her savings to herself, Subhasini might have lived in a better house and had more possessions. But, she says, "What's the use of material things like bangles and saris. We can't take them with us when we die. But, the happy faces of the cured poor people have given me such joy and meaning in this life."

Three years ago, Ajoy persuaded her to stop selling vegetables. She was getting old; her knees were giving her trouble. She now tends to the sick in the hospital. She says, "This hospital means everything to me. It is my wealth, my knowledge and my happiness."

But, her mission is not yet over. "Only when this hospital becomes a full-fledged 24-hour hospital can I die happy," she concludes.

BIOGRAPHER

Anita Pratap is a Karmaveer Puraskaar award recipient and is an expatriate Indian writer and journalist. In 1983, she was the first journalist who interviewed LTTE chief V Prabhakaran. She won the George Polk award for television reporting of the takeover of Kabul by the Taliban. She was also the India bureau chief for CNN.

The panacea for all our social ills lies in ordinary everyday heroes.

– Jeroninio

God of Small, Simple but Significant Actions

Chewang Norphel

Chewang Norphel makes glaciers. Nobody taught him, he just learnt how to do it by observing nature. And then, this 'glacier man' used his technique to transform the lives of the farmers of his impoverished village.

Born in 1936 to Tibetan parents, Chewang hails from Skara village, 2.5 kilometers away from Leh in Ladakh, India's remote and northern-most region. All 100 families of his village have traditionally been subsistence farmers, cultivating wheat, barley, mustard and peas. As a child, he tended cows and yaks, while his father tilled the hard and crusty soil. Tucked away in the Himalayas between Pakistan and China, Ladakh is a sweeping expanse of land, rich in history, stark in beauty, colorful in culture and awe-inspiring in its Buddhist heritage.

But, misery clouded this Shangri La. Ladakh's greatest enemy is neither its remoteness nor its winter chill, but it's aridity. It's a treacherous case of scarcity amidst abundance. Melting snow generates millions of gallons of water. But, as it flows into the mountain streams too late in the year, most of the water goes waste. Understandably, nothing grows in Ladakh in winter as it's too cold. Cultivation is limited to the extremely short season of spring and summer warmth. Spring arrives in April but by the time the great Himalayan glaciers melt to fill the mountain streams, it is June.

Too much, too late!

Ladakhi farmers need water in April to first moisten the dry, winter chapped fields. Then they can plough and plant the seeds. And then in June, the fields can be watered by the gurgling mountain streams. This is the perfect, natural cycle that would enable the local villagers to farm their fields properly. Except there is no water in April because the glaciers are still frozen. This predicament trapped the villagers in a perennial cycle of poverty. They were forced to wait until June to moisten, plough and plant the seeds. All this had to be rushed through in a compressed timeframe. Thus, the earth was not sufficiently prepared, dooming the fields to low and erratic yields, even crop failures.

If only the villagers could get water in April! For Chewang, it became an obsession to sit in his garden during his holidays and ponder over this conundrum, while idly watching the water drip to the ground from the lone village tap. The tap had to be kept open in winter to let the water flow through so that it did not freeze and burst the pipe. So, the water dripped away, wasting into the earth, forming a large pool that became a sheet of ice in winter.

Eureka!

That's how Chewang hit upon his simple but brilliant idea. What if he stored the plentiful water from the melted snow some place close to the village all through summer and autumn so that it could form a glacier in winter? This man-made glacier would then melt in spring to provide the much needed water for the villagers at the right time. The natural Himalayan glaciers were located at about 18,000 feet. The solution would be to form glaciers near their villages at about 13,000 feet so that it would melt earlier in the year, and thus provide water for his villagers in April.

The idea struck him in 1987. A junior engineer in the Jammu and Kashmir government's rural department, Chewang put the knowledge gained from his Lucknow civil engineering diploma course, local work experience, and resources to translate his idea into action on a trial basis in water-starved Phutse village, 80 kilometers away from Skarra. He dug and built diversion canals to channel the water from the main mountain streams to suitable water catchment sites about four kilometers away from the village. He designed the reservoirs in a series of steppe formations, locating them in mountain shade so that the water would remain frozen in winter to form large glaciers. From the glacier, feeder canals took the water back to the natural mountain streams that irrigated the villages.

The idea worked. As the glaciers were located lower down, they melted early and the villagers started getting water in April when they needed it most.

Nature created a problem. But, it was Chewang's genius that he found the solution too in nature. No idea is great unless it is simple. Chewang's low-cost glaciers turned out to be an ingenious way of solving a perennial problem. The Phutse glacier cost ₹ 90,000. Local villagers did the manual work and the materials used were entirely local – stones, rocks and earth. Thus, the solution was both inexpensive and environmentally sound.

Chewang has now built seven glaciers, the smallest being 500 feet-long in Umla to the largest being the two kilometer long in Phutse. Depending on the topography, the width of the glacier ranges from 50 to 200 feet; the depth from two to seven feet.

Restoring the viability of rural farming has many unseen and long-term benefits. It stems the tide of rural displacement. Poverty has driven away so many young men and women from their pristine villages to the degrading slums of the towns nearby and cities far away. Keeping villagers rooted to their farmlands not only ensures a safer, healthier and better life for them, but also helps to preserve the local Tibetan culture and Buddhist heritage.

As a government servant, Chewang could not change the world or even his state. But, he changed his local environment, using whatever little expertise and resources he had. Unlike millions of others, he was not content to merely draw a salary. He wanted to use his position, education, skills and experience to improve the lives of the people around him. His constant interaction with the people very early in his career convinced him that water scarcity was public enemy number one in his homeland. So, he used his job to tackle the problem. As a civil engineer, he built tanks, bridges, irrigation canals and other public works that have made life easier for the local inhabitants. During his career, he built over 300 canals, some of them in tough, stony terrain comprising vertical rocks, to irrigate 20,000 acres and benefiting 75 percent of Leh's 1,17,000 inhabitants. He had to make do with little money and rudimentary equipment for digging and blasting. He had to coax villagers to volunteer their labor. But, his determination compensated shortages and inadequate facilities. He recalls building the first suspension wooden bridge in the arid Zanskar area. There was no timber available as the high altitude does not permit vegetation. He had to transport the logs of wood and rocks manually and on mules. The villagers at first refused to lift the boulders, as they were heavy. So, Chewang carried them himself, shaming the others to join in.

After he retired from government service, Chewang took up a job as the project engineer of the Leh Nutrition Project, an NGO set up in 1979 by Britain's Save the Children Fund. With funding now coming from several national and international agencies, the project has expanded its activities to cover child education and empowerment, watershed development programs and HIV/AIDS.

Chewang needs no studies to convince him of the threat of global warming. With growing alarm, he watches the mighty Himalayan glaciers shrink and recede further from his village with every passing year. In his childhood, the Stok glacier covered half the distant mountain range that rimmed his horizon. Now, the glacier is a mere icing on the crest. He yearns to restore the ice caps by building more glaciers. And he sees the urgent need to build reservoirs in every one of Leh's 112 villages to harness the water instead of letting it all go waste into the mighty Indus River in autumn. India, he notes, spends ₹ 2 crores a day on maintaining its troops on the Siachen glacier. One day's military expenditure on this icy wasteland could build 50 glaciers in Ladakh!

Simple ideas spring from the well of deep commitment. Chewang was committed to solving his people's distress. He brooded day and night, and one day, the penny dropped. Simple ideas transform lives. They challenge one's blasé assumptions, one's whole way of thinking. Hadn't we assumed that technology and innovations are the domains of the geeks? Hadn't we assumed that interventions to improve the lives of ordinary people are expensive and complex? Hadn't we cynically assumed that nothing can be done to bring tangible public benefits? Hadn't we assumed that only God makes glaciers?

In his own little way, Chewang is a God of small, simple but significant actions. After all, Buddhism states, God dwells within us.

But, Chewang sees no grandeur, let alone divinity in his achievements. He remains simple and unassuming even after winning accolades and prestigious national and international awards. What does he think helped him to succeed in his efforts? Says he with alacrity: "People's cooperation". You have to make people share your vision, participate in your dream. "Without people's cooperation, you cannot achieve anything," he adds.

BIOGRAPHER

Anita Pratap is a Karmaveer Puraskaar award recipient and is an expatriate Indian writer and journalist. In 1983, she was the first journalist who interviewed LTTE chief V. Prabhakaran. She won the George Polk award for television reporting of the takeover of Kabul by the Taliban. She was also the India bureau chief for CNN.

During a lecture in B-schools on ethical leadership, I once told students to get together the next day to clean the streets. While most students agreed, some did not. One even told me that he will not do this as he is an intellectual. I replied: "Not to worry, my friend. I always wanted to be an intellectual too, but since I never quite made it, I shall clean the streets with other students," and then went out and cleaned the streets.

– Jeroninio

The Voice of the Voiceless

Fr George Pulikuthiyil

For ten years, Gopi's parents preserved his corpse in a tub of formalin in their thatched house in Kerala's coastal town of Chertalla. They did this, not out of grief, but out of anger. They believed their 23-year-old son Gopi had been tortured to death in police custody. They vowed they would not cremate him until they got justice.

Three years into their vigil, justice arrived in the form of a catholic priest-cum-lawyer – Father George Pulikuthiyil, who had read about this bizarre incident in a newspaper and headed straight to Chertalla and volunteered to file a court case for free. He recalls, "This was astonishing news. I couldn't believe the agony of the parents watching over their son's dead body every day."

Evidently, local rivalry had led to the police falsely accusing Gopi of stealing a transistor radio. Two days after he was picked up from home by local constables, Gopi was found dead with abdominal wounds. The police claimed he had attempted suicide by stabbing himself with a broken tube light. Fr George exposed the holes in this version and fought a tortuous court battle. He won in 1998. Gopi's parents got ₹ 3 lakhs in compensation and they finally cremated their beloved son.

The legal victory in this sensational case was a high point in the tumultuous life of Fr George. Lured by the prospects of acquiring free higher education in a seminary, he left his remote village in Wayanad to bustling Thrissur, to become a priest in 1965. He was 12-years-old. In the seminary, reading about the martyrdom of Christian missionaries, who worked for the poor in China and South Africa, fired his imagination. Unconsciously, 'live dangerously, die heroically' became his motto.

In 1981, he was ordained a priest and began working at the Chavara Cultural Centre in Ernakulam. He soon realized that monastic life bored him. He felt isolated from human condition, distanced from the everyday struggles of the ordinary people whom he yearned to serve. For him, priesthood meant reliving the life of Jesus Christ. Serving the poor appealed to him much more than being cloistered, listening to the tedious confessions of people who committed the same sins – lying, cheating, disobeying. His work at the Centre sensitized him to the injustice that the poor had to cope with. Reminisces Fr George: "I was convinced that God was not confined to the chapel. He existed amidst the people, in their struggles, in their miseries. It's out there I knew I would find God." And thus, the second motto in his life was born: 'Defend the defenceless.'

The best way to do that was to become a lawyer and fight for the rights of the oppressed. And so, Fr George headed to Mumbai where he did a course in law. Gopi's was the very first case he fought. And it brought him enormous personal satisfaction. A string of cases followed. In 1992, a year after he first took on Gopi's case, Fr George started Jananeethi, an NGO, to provide justice to the poor. It offered free legal aid and even fought cases in court. Recalls Fr George, "Cases began pouring in."

But then, so did the complaints. Most of his court cases were against the rich – landowners for usurping the land of the poor, industrialists for arbitrarily dismissing workers or businessmen for illegally converting agricultural land for commercial use. The litigating priest became a threat to the 'vested interests' – politicians, landed gentry and factory owners, who across the world wield tremendous clout with the Church through their donations, connections and goodwill.

Relations between Fr George and the Church began to sour. Fr George believed in Liberation Theology, a brand of priestly activism that swept across the Catholic Church all over the world in the 1980s and 1990s. Priests were going out of the confines of their churches and seminaries to fight for the rights of the poor. The Vatican frowned on them and the movement petered out. The bruised relations culminated with Fr George and the church parting ways at the turn of the century. From Fr George, he became George.

He had to drop his prefix, but he did not drop his calling or his faith. He says, "Priesthood is service, not a designation. Worship isn't about fiddling with prayer beads or kneeling in church. Every act I do is a prayer. I believe in Gandhi's philosophy that the best way to worship is to oppose evil. I don't believe in religion anymore, but I believe in God. Not a God that is male, stern, destroyer of enemies or hostile to other religions. God is present everywhere, in everyone, in everything. God is love, mercy, truth, compassion."

And so his days bustled with prayer. He plunged into work. Through Jananeethi, he fought for the rights of all sections of society, irrespective of caste, class and creed. He filed cases involving human rights abuses, gender injustice, caste discrimination, domestic violence, dowry cases and protecting the rights of HIV patients, handicapped persons and children. Recognizing his contribution, the Kerala government eventually appointed him chairman of the Child Welfare Committee for a three-year term. The welfare of orphans and neglected, abandoned or abused children in Thrissur became his responsibility.

Rewards came, but so did calumny. Death threats, character assassination, allegations and accusations were hurled at him. But, he lived through it all, keeping his sanity and his dignity intact. The late 1990s was especially bad. He recalls, "I woke up every day thinking, today may be my last day. Let me make the most of it. And at night, when I went to bed, I felt it was a miracle, I have lived another day." What kept him going through all these troubles was his passion to connect with the struggles of the poor, to contribute his bit to help them achieve their rights and live a life of dignity, and his conviction that above all, he must be honest to himself and to the needy people around him, in word and in deed.

Fr George demonstrated the healing power of justice. Jananeethi's Psycho-Legal Therapeutic Services, especially for victims of torture and organized violence, attracted international attention. Protecting the environment is another issue that is close to Fr George's heart. He has continuously sought to preserve the unspoilt beauty of Kerala's dense forests and verdant hills. Few know that it was he who first took up investigations against Coca Cola's factory in Plachimada in Palakkad. Jananeethi published a report that exposed how toxic slurry was being used as fertilizer, poisoning the land and underground water. *Down to Earth,* a New Delhi-based environment magazine, picked up the report and it was followed by a major expose by the BBC and other media and NGO organizations, eventually culminating in Kerala government banning the sale of Coca Cola.

In 2000, Fr George scored another major victory when following his tireless efforts, Thichur in Thrissur was declared India's first litigation-free village. Teachers and students of Thrissur's Government Law College went around Thichur compiling all the disputes and court cases filed from the village. Thereafter, a committee of eminent persons heard the cases and resolved them by mediating between the parties. Almost all the pending 264 cases were settled. People found it cheaper, quicker and less troublesome to settle disputes this way, instead of taking the police-lawyer-court route. Says Fr George, "This is how disputes were resolved in the olden days. It works because the whole community functions as a team."

Avoidance of litigation, however, does not translate into absence of crime. In 2004, Fr George decided to take one more ambitious step – to make Ward 12 of Thrissur crime-free. Says Fr George, "This sounds utopian, but I believe it's possible because people are inherently good and want to lead a hassle-free life." He points out that crime is usually the result of poverty, unemployment, homelessness, displacement, communal divisions, political polarization, lack of infrastructure, administrative corruption, diseases, sexual offences, drug abuse and mental illness. He adds, "Freedom from crime means freedom from fear and want. Justice, equality and Rule of Law are paramount. It involves fair and equitable development that ensures the welfare of all. Jesus called this society the Kingdom of God, Mahatma Gandhi called it Ram Rajya, Plato and Marx called it the Welfare Society and we in legal terms call it the Egalitarian Society. Call it what you want, but the message is the same: peace and harmony cannot be achieved in society without justice and equality."

Fr George acknowledges that realizing his dream is easier said than done. The lack of funds to do noble work is the single biggest impediment. Another is the rampant disunity within the society. Echoing a popular sentiment,

Fr George notes: "There is always a group of people in the society who won't work themselves and what is even worse, won't allow others to work. So, they keep raising obstacles and spreading venom." This can be frustrating, even disheartening. But, he says the one lesson he has learnt in life is: "Commitment makes the difference. If you stay committed, nothing can pull you back from your goal."

BIOGRAPHER

Anita Pratap is a Karmaveer Puraskaar award recipient and is an expatriate Indian writer and journalist. In 1983, she was the first journalist who interviewed LTTE chief V. Prabhakaran. She won the George Polk award for television reporting of the takeover of Kabul by the Taliban. She was also the India bureau chief for CNN.

Courage is so rare nowadays that one gets cornered for having the courage of conviction and living by one's ideals. However, it is great to be cornered, since the corner with courage is never too crowded.

– Jeroninio

The Princess and the Pirate

Gregory David Roberts

In January 1997, a twenty-year period of my life led as a fugitive and behind bars came to an end, when I was released from prison for the last time, with one dollar and forty-three cents in my pocket. While some of the contemporaries from my university days were already moving into early retirement, I was reconstructing my life from the rubble of my own crimes and the disfiguring cruelties of various national justice systems. In fact, I did have certain plans in mind, and I was determined to see them through, but one over-arching dream encompassed all of them: to return to Mumbai, India, and to take whatever steps I could to make a positive difference in the lives of some of the city's most disadvantaged people.

After seven years of work, and after my novel, *Shantaram*, was published and the movie rights sold to Johnny Depp, Warner Brothers and the brilliant producer, Graham King, I had sufficient money to take care of the needs of my family and to return to Mumbai, to realize the dream that had sustained me.

In early 2004, after talking with many friends in the island city of Mumbai, I decided that the project I'd like to invest in – the project that was the best fit for me as a man who loved the unparalleled sensation of freedom that fills the heart when you ride a motorcycle, and for the community of South Mumbai where I'd spent so many years – was a bicycle and motorcycle repair shop, which could give training and job-skills to men who lived on the streets of the city. The shop was called *Happy Cycles*, and its aim was to give the men a skill-set that would allow them to find work anywhere in the country, and to be self-supporting from that point onward – the *teach a man to fish, instead of giving him a fish* principle.

At around the same time that I was setting up my association with the *Happy Cycles* team, a royal Princess from Europe, Her Serene Highness Princess Francoise Sturdza, was following a dream of her own: a dream that led her to the Malabar Coast, then to Cochin, and finally to Chennai, in South India.

Princess Francoise, who through marriage to the Sturdza family of Moldavia, which eventually became part of modern-day Romania, had been invited to Romania after the fall of the dictator, Ceausescu. The Princess and her friends and relatives witnessed there the most appalling condition and intolerable neglect of orphans, deprived children and abandoned elderly people.

Although a titled Princess, Francoise Sturdza is a hard-working woman, who built two companies from the ground up, single-handedly, and made those companies thriving successes in the closed, conservative and almost exclusively male world of business in Geneva, Switzerland. When she saw the terribly disturbing conditions of orphans and the abandoned elderly in Ceausescu's Romania, she put her managerial mind to work on finding a sustainable solution.

Working with Princess Margareta of Romania Foundation, Princess Francoise devised a plan to fund a facility that could provide a safe haven for abandoned elderly people, and at the same time arrange child-minding facilities for neglected children. A suitable building was found, bought and transformed to house the abandoned elderly people in one wing, and gave the elderly people the opportunity to care for the children of single parent and other struggling families in a separate wing. A legal service operated from the facility to give advice on pensions (which in many cases had been illegally denied) and other rights of the elderly people, and as social service taught computer skills and connected the residents to social support and entertainment services.

After reading an influential book on the history of Vasco da Gama's travels to the Malabar Coast of India, Princess Francoise decided to visit the centres mentioned in the book. When she arrived in Cochin, she established herself there in a pied-a-terre apartment, explored the regions of South India and finally settled into an apartment in Chennai.

Some members of the committee that had worked to build the facility in Romania, inspired by the work that had excited their passion for so many months, asked Princess Francoise to find another charitable project. With her heart now putting down roots in India, Princess Francoise agreed to create another project, but only in India. The committee members agreed, and after many meetings with a talented Indian team to decide on a suitable project, the Hope For India Foundation was established in 2005.

The Hope for India Foundation decided to 'adopt' one of the most distressed schools, home to 500 children, in the greater Chennai district, and transform it into a model school. Using the medical expertise of a team from the University Hospital of Geneva, a complete analysis of the nutritional status of the 500 children was undertaken. The team discovered that a significant percentage of the students were malnourished, and also that many students returned home during the lunch period because they had no meal at school. The Hope for India Foundation and the University Hospital medical team created a nutritional snacks program, providing free snacks for all the children of the school, *provided they stayed at school and finished their day's studies.*

With the truancy problem and nutritional deficiencies solved, the Hope for India committee set about raising the living conditions within the school grounds. There were no toilets – none at all – for the 500 school children, and the smell of faeces and urine filled all of the classrooms. There were no taps providing drinking water – in fact, there was no drinking water at all at the school. And the open 'assembly area' was a deep, muddy quagmire for half of the year, and a dusty desert for the other half.

The Foundation constructed water tanks, arranged for weekly deliveries of eatables and then installed a filtration unit to provide clean drinking water. The Foundation built toilet blocks with septic tank systems, installed long basins with multiple drinking fountains and paved the assembly area. Turning their attention to the teaching staff, the Foundation agreed with the school council and parents that the hiring of new teachers – something beyond the limited school budget – was urgently necessary. The Foundation paid for the hiring of five new teachers, two ladies to cook and prepare food on new gas-fired stoves (instead of the extremely smoky wooden fires previously used), two cleaning ladies and two security watchmen to protect the new facilities installed in the school from opportunistic thieves.

A sports teacher was engaged by the Foundation – an inspiration of Princess Francoise – to teach the children yoga, sports, and general physical health. The sports teacher instilled a school spirit in the hearts of the children, and within a short time the students were representing their school for the first time in inter-school sports events. As a part of the combined sports and social program, the children were encouraged to understand that they had all rights under law of more privileged children, and had every right to expect the chance to be all that they could be in life. The school has, indeed, become a model school. The school roll has expanded to 1,000 children, and representatives of schools from all over India – and from as far away as Bangladesh and the Middle East – have visited the school to discover how they can duplicate the success. The Hope for India Foundation itself changed during the process: the committee that 'adopted' a very distressed school with almost no trace of hope, and helped that school to become a source of hope for other schools, decided that it had passed through the 'hope' phase, and changed its name to the Heart for India Foundation.

The Heart for India Foundation has scaled-up its operations in India to include another school in the greater Chennai area, one with 2,000 students, and two orphanages for abandoned girl children, called Girls Town One and Girls Town Two. Using the model where a sponsor donates all of the administrative costs of the Foundation (a model developed by Princess Francoise from her business experience), Heart for India can ensure that 100 cents in every dollar donated to the charitable foundation reaches the children who benefit from the projects. The Foundation is going from strength to strength, and is opening new projects in Mumbai, in 2013.

During this period of several years, beginning in 2005, my own work with my much smaller charity continued in Mumbai. From one motorcycle and bicycle repair business, providing training, paid work and decent conditions to pavement-dwellers with families, we've expanded to three shops, and a combined staff of 30 men. My charity exists completely from my own resources, and I don't ask for or accept donations from any source, business or private.

I met Princess Francoise at a Gala Dinner in Mumbai's Taj Mahal hotel, at the end of 2005, while we were both heavily engaged in our independent social projects. As fate would have it, we were seated opposite at a table reserved for foreigners who do charity work in India. We were introduced to one another, and the dialogue that became the continuing story of our lives began with a discussion of our mutual passion for positive projects, focusing on building and rebuilding the dignity of human beings suffering in extreme circumstances. We began to work together, meeting in Mumbai and Geneva several times a year. Some years into that collaborative work, I proposed to Princess Francoise in Mumbai, after a long day of work together on a social justice project in a South Mumbai slum. In 2008, we were married, and we continue to work together closely on all of our social projects.

When the iCONGO committee notified me that I had been nominated for a Karmaveer Puraskaar award for social justice and citizen action, I replied in writing, stating that although I was honoured to be nominated, my wife was a much more deserving nominee. I sent background material on the work done by Princess Francoise and the Heart for India Foundation committee, and invited the iCONGO committee to transfer my nomination to Princess Francoise.

The committee replied, saying: "We agree with you, Mr Roberts – your wife, Princess Francoise, is a more deserving nominee – but we would like to inform you that we are nominating *both* of you for the award." In due course, both my wife and I were proud and honoured recipients of the Karmaveer Puraskaar, and we attended the awards ceremony in New Delhi. It was one of the happiest moments of our lives, and one that we will always treasure.

In part because of the inspiration sparked by the iCONGO committee, the indefatigable and charismatic Jeroninio Almeida in person and the work done by all of the other award recipients, I've extended my own work to include support for Doctors Without Borders, The Elders, the UNITE charity group, the Zeitz Foundation for Intercultural Ecosphere Safety, Human Rights Watch and the World Health Organization, among others. The single spark from iCONGO lit a prairie fire in my heart, and each new opportunity to do what little I can, to contribute my small measure of worth to the great cause of social justice, inspires my commitment with fresh ardour.

For her part, Princess Francoise is developing new programs that can bring her experience as a successful business woman, in a business world dominated by men, to young women in Mumbai who have limited means, but who have the ambition to be all that they can be.

The coda to this summary of who we are, and what we do as Karmaveer Puraskaar recipients is that there are many friends and acquaintances in Mumbai – and indeed across the world – who refer to us as 'The Princess and The Pirate.' And it's true that the two worlds of a titled Princess and a 'writer of fortune,' as one magazine called me, are as far apart as any that exist in this world. And in the normal course of events, our paths would never have crossed, and no imagined destiny would've seen us love one another.

But we did meet, and we did love and we continue to work together on our social projects. And the thing that brought us together – that shaped the contours of our two destinies into intersecting and intertwining paths – was the decision we both made to do what we could to work for social justice, to try to make a positive difference and to be the change that we want to see in the world. That one step toward the Light can become the leap that carries your heart across continents, as it did for us, in the most important and fulfilling journey life grants to any of us.

BIOGRAPHER

Gregory David Roberts is a consultant, philosopher, movie producer, global ambassador for human rights organizations and an Australian author best known for his international bestselling novel *Shantaram*.

We keep waiting for another mahatma to make a difference. It is time to stop waiting. The mantra is 'I change to change India'. Each one of us is the mahatma and has the power to change our nation.

– Jeroninio

Together, We Can

Lakshman Singh

The broken bund (mud embankment) was emblematic of all that was wrong with Laporia. The inhabitants of this arid village in an arid district in India's most arid state, Rajasthan, were dirt poor. They were malnourished, wore torn clothes and rarely washed. Soap, they could not afford. Neither sugar nor milk in their tea. Many went to bed hungry every night. Diseases and illnesses went untreated, because there were no medicines. Children remained illiterate. Cattle died of thirst. Upper and lower castes crumbling property, dragged relatives to court.

The root cause of Laporia's misery was acute water scarcity.

Farming was the main occupation for the 200 families. But drought, compounded by the crumbling bund, dry ponds and empty wells, doomed cultivation to a perennial losing battle with nature. City jobs, thus, were the sole meal ticket. Lakshman Singh went to Jaipur to study, but dropped out of school because his family could not afford the fees. Depressed, he returned to the misery of his village. He faced a bleak future. No education meant no job in the city; no water meant no farming in his village.

Lakshman was 18-years-old when he realized the only way to turn Laporia's misfortune was to repair the bund along the dry pond. It had remained broken for 30 years. If scanty rainfall could be collected in the pond, then feeder canals could be dug to irrigate the fields, making cultivation feasible. Laporia could turn green. Villagers mocked his fantasy. "And who would pay our wages to repair the bund?" they demanded sarcastically. Lakshman had no answer. He was stumped: no rich landlords to subsidize the labour; no philanthropists nearby to fund them and the government was far away and unconcerned. He was thoroughly depressed. There seemed no way out of this vicious cycle.

Then one day, it struck him perhaps there is a way out: villagers could volunteer to repair the bund. After all, they were the beneficiaries. Neighbors scoffed at his suggestion. They had better things to do. Lakshman hence, resolved to do it himself. One friend supported him. The pair decided to repair the bund themselves. It was no small task: the bund was 1.5 kilometers long and 15 feet high. Armed with spades, they set off to the bund one summer day in 1978. Passersby wondered, "How can the bund be repaired by just two people?" Lakshman retorted, "Well, you can join us, and that would help." Four village youths joined him. By the seventh day, the trickle swelled to 20. When rains came two months later, water collected in the pond for the first time in decades.

By 1984, the pond was irrigating 1,800 acres of farmland. From virtually no income, the average income of a family rose to ₹ 14,000 per annum – enough to provide a comfortable life. Villagers congregated for the ceremony to name the pond 'Anna Sagar', the sea of grain. Asserts Lakshman, "If you really want to achieve anything in life, you have to get down and do it yourself. You can lead others only by setting an example."

Lakshman also devised a simple but unique water harvesting program in the outskirts of his village. He calls it the *chauka* system. It comprises of a series of channels and square pits fringed by two-foot-high bunds in a chequer board pattern over a five-kilometer expanse in which rainwater collects and meanders down the natural slope of the land. This not only enables the water to flow into the ponds nearby, but also creates grassy patches on the pits on which cattle can graze. Thus, his dry wastelands bordering the villages were converted into grassy village common land, ideal for pasture.

Villages die when common land disappears. Called *gochar*, pasture is considered sacred by Hindu villagers. Across India, pasture for cattle grazing is vanishing, either due to drought or to land grabbers. Grassy *gochar* symbolizes healthy villages. It symbolizes the symbiotic relationship between man, nature and animals. If water is harvested, crops and grass grow and cattle have natural vegetation to feed on, which is cheaper and healthier than hormone-injected cattle feed. More cattle means more dung, which is the cheapest and best natural fertilizer-cum-pesticide. Organic farming – which now the world acknowledges – is the healthy, and natural way to cultivate crops. There is no place for pesticides and fertilizers that poison the earth and drive farmers to penury. Says Lakshman, "The less we interfere with nature, the better it is for all of us. Everything and everyone have their place in our eco-system. We live in a natural cycle of inter-dependence – land, water, man, beast, all depend on each other. If you don't disrupt the cycle of dependency and this natural bio-rhythm, there will be harmony."

Over the years, all the ponds of the village were rejuvenated. Villagers performed *puja* (rites) to celebrate the consecration of 'Dev Sagar' and 'Phool Sagar'. Crops were harvested twice a year. Laporia became virtually self-sufficient as farmers grew corn, maize, bajra, jowar, wheat, lentils, groundnuts, chillies, mustard, fenugreek and variety of vegetables.

Their new-found sense of well-being made villagers feel the need to organize a thanksgiving ceremony. In 1987, the villagers institutionalized their annual nature-worshipping ritual. Villagers gather to renew their bond with nature and each other, eat *gud* (melted jaggery), tie sacred threads and apply *tilak* on trees, birds, cattle, wells and ponds. They pray to Lord Indra to bless the village with rain. They tie *rakhi* on each other as a mark of friendship and community-bonding. It is a day of festivity and rejoicing.

From an impoverished, drought-afflicted, conflict-ridden village, Laporia became a trail-blazing symbol of rural renewal, a self-sufficient oasis of agricultural produce, peace and harmony. Its fame spread. Other adjoining villages followed suit. Villagers started organizing the *Shram Dhan*, to donate their labour to desilt the tanks and ponds. The desilting ceremony takes about five days. Over the years, this became a vibrant local tradition. Inhabitants of Laporia went on a *padayatra* to the adjoining villages to help with the desilting of ponds. These villagers came to theirs. Now, 500 villages participate in these *padayatras* to desilt their water bodies. In the evening, youngsters organize cultural entertainment – songs, dances and street theatre. The evening ends with a sumptuous feast prepared by the village's housewives. Says Lakshman, "As businessmen and officers, my classmates make more money than me. But, I have the satisfaction of changing the life of my entire village."

Village development committees now decide on new programs to build roads, install taps, and establish health and education facilities. Self-sufficiency is the village mantra; Panchayati Raj as Mahatma Gandhi envisioned. "Villagers must be encouraged to become custodians of their village and its surroundings. If every village becomes a viable, harmonious and peaceful economic unit, then people would be happy and India would be strong. When village life breaks down, and youngsters are forced to migrate in search of work, then villages starve and cities bloat. Both will die. "It's not sustainable," predicts Lakshman, who has never heard of the pro-environment Norwegian Prime Minister, Gro Harlem Brundtland, who coined the phrase 'sustainable development' in the 1980s. Lakshman, typifies the Indian villager, who blessed with robust common sense, needs no celebrity endorsements or academic studies to convince him of the ancient wisdom that he carries in his genes, refreshed everyday by observing nature.

One would have expected Lakshman to be rewarded with a bouquet of citations for path-breaking work. Instead, village officials were displeased. They served him with a show-cause notice for usurping their authority. Lakshman had framed new rules for his village. If a villager cut one tree, he would have to plant five saplings as compensation. If he hunted animals, he must pay a fine of 11 bushels of grain. If he shot a bird, he would have to feed the village birds. Most complied; some complained. Local officials were annoyed. Punishing villagers was their job, not his. Lakshman was summoned to their office, but his entreaties and explanations that *patwaris* ignored such offences or took bribes from the offenders and released them, fell on deaf ears.

When he heard about this harassment, a botanist from Jaipur, who had taken an interest in Laporia's transformation, contacted New Delhi-based scientists, who in turn urged village officials to lay off Lakshman. They did. Slowly, brickbats turned to bouquets as the authorities began to reward him with prizes for his pioneering work to rejuvenate Laporia.

Perhaps, the most remarkable aspect about Laporia's renewal is its forestation that has lured birds. Says Lakshman with pride, "Birds are the best signs of a healthy environment." Varieties of birds now flock to Laporia. The village courtyard is a daily *Kumbh mela* of parrots, peacocks perched on roof tops, woodpeckers hugging trees, pigeons strutting and koels cooing hauntingly. People of this once arid, godforsaken village greet each day with the birdsong of larks, warblers, nightingales and other winged minstrels of the forests.

BIOGRAPHER

Anita Pratap is a Karmaveer Puraskaar award recipient and is an expatriate Indian writer and journalist. In 1983, she was the first journalist who interviewed LTTE chief V Prabhakaran. She won the George Polk award for television reporting of the takeover of Kabul by the Taliban. She was also the India bureau chief for CNN.

A life of dignity is not the prerogative of the privileged, but the birthright of every individual.

– Jeroninio

Ek Tara – Wings to Dream and Fly

Geeta Puri

"We are what we repeatedly do. Excellence, therefore, is not an act but a habit."

– Aristotle

Aristotle, it seems, had a different world in mind. While India shines as one of the fastest growing democracies in the world, internally, it has never been as segmented as we find it today. A disconnected social structure together with the unfortunate selfish stance of some men threatens to derail this great nation. What is even most disheartening is that while Indian history is filled with stories of great sacrifices and human triumph, it seems to not repeat itself within the Indian context. These are just some of the thoughts that tormented Geeta Puri as she wandered into the world of 'non-profit' work. She felt disappointed at the growing difference between the potential this country possessed and the reality that was starting to take a stronger hold.

"He who wished to secure the good of others, has already secured his own," Geeta remarks. "This quote by Confucius is not merely a beautiful combination of words, but a life stance for me. Since I started *Ek Tara*, I have devoted myself fully to the cause of securing social justice and equality for our country's underprivileged children and women. What started as a personal 'give-back' to society has now turned into an established and recognized effort to empower the

120

next generation with the right skills and confidence to hold their head high and dream bigger."

As an entrepreneur, Geeta made her presence felt through her brand 'Gloss' within the local t-shirt market. A hit with the youth, her role as lead designer took her regularly to multiple cities around India, as she came across people from various walks of life. As a result, having worked in the business world all her life, jumping the fence seemed unreal at first, but she quickly learned that NGOs functioned in a far more cut-throat world than she first thought. The myriad set of formal obligations that needed to be completed and the obscure rules that prohibited fundraising were all mind-numbing. One is compelled to wonder that if doing a good deed requires so much bureaucracy, then why one should even bother! If we believe that culture is a learned behavior, then we, it seems, have learned to ignore problems in the hope that they will go away instead of facing them. Geeta feels that though people choose to ignore the presence of social stratification – a problem deep rooted in India – and want to wish it away, still exists in every corner of our society.

Geeta's journey into *Ek Tara* is by no means the typical path of salvation most great leaders seem to follow. She was fortunate enough to have lived a comfortable life and thus cannot boast of any real life-changing experiences of her more established peers. However, as an outsider looking in, her story is far more personal as it took roots in her emotional state of being at the time and hence is far more inspirational. Having been brought up in a household that did not struggle to make ends meet, she was never fully exposed to the harsher realities of life, particularly in India. While poverty and social injustice were known to her conceptually, she and others around her from similar backgrounds remained somewhat aloof to the depth of this reality as well as its detrimental effects on the welfare of those subjected to it. I believe, Geeta's experience reflects a natural extension of growing up in a democracy where a government that is for and by the people is just expected to function efficiently. Today, the dramatic growth in the number of NGOs with varying levels of success have at the very least made it harder for those who simply wish to escape this unfortunate truth and remain within their bubbles.

However, Geeta does not shy away from confessing that her life was very similar to that described above. It seems that while she tried to do her little bit like a responsible citizen, she was by no means as committed to the cause of social improvement as she is today. Her busy business schedule was only minimally supplemented with her work at a local NGO called Samarpan, dedicated to the overall upbringing of neglected children and where she participated in workshops for life-skill training. It was a turning point in her life as her heart became more involved with the time she spent with children. However, at that time, she decided not to pursue her newfound desire, given the mounting pressure on the business front. While her work got the better of her, the seed had already been planted and as it would become clear later on, her heart never left Samarpan.

What changed things for her was a minor corrective surgery that turned into a traumatic incident, leaving her utterly helpless. She strove to use the resources bestowed on her by the grace of God to make her life just a little more comfortable. However, this time around, life had other plans and forced her into an indefinite state of discomfort post the surgery of her eyes. Today, she finds it quite ironic that what we use to turn away at the sight of something unappealing is exactly what started to hurt her and for once she could not turn away. This marked a critical turning point in her life. Geeta says that in her times of pain and frustration, "No amount of money could rid me of this tortuous state of constant discomfort. I felt disappointed when I read the words of Mother Teresa who said that, 'I try to give to the poor people for love what the rich could get for money'." It made her realize that her pain may in fact be trivial in comparison to the horrors faced by the underprivileged in our society.

It is this feeling of helplessness together with the revival of the intense passion she felt during her time at Samarpan that slowly made her think of the state of our society and those who are a part of it. It particularly made her think of all those individuals who live their entire lives without even having a fair chance to do anything against those who violate their basic human rights, while the privileged few mourn the slightest of discomforts! The deeper she thought, the more strongly she started to feel about doing something for those who really did need help and support.

Thus, she took it upon herself to try and make a difference, however small, in the lives of the helpless. Geeta's decision to fully dedicate herself to the improvement of the society was clearly a selfless act. Her mission was to make a tangible difference. However, she insists, "I maintain realistic assumptions with regard to what I can achieve. I strongly believe in the mantra that any difference, if positive, is a noteworthy one." As a result, she focuses more on making qualitative differences instead of quantitative, as the latter approach rarely achieves successful outcomes.

Geeta wanted to be involved in the development of an idea and as a result, needed someone who shared her beliefs and goals for the future of the foundation. Geeta found these qualities in Jaya, her partner and close friend.

"Having observed the two partners at work, I sensed a deep chemistry that existed between the two, a bond secured by the motivation to develop *Ek Tara*," she explains. Since the beginning, Jaya reflected a strong enthusiasm for the project, sharing the same goals as Geeta, which made it a lot easier for them to work together. In her words: "I believe in her as much as she believes in me and together we strive towards a successful outcome to this project."

Ek Tara was started with the idea of providing hope to the underprivileged youth in an attempt to help them realize their potential. Its purpose was to fill the gaps in the lives of these children, education taking top priority, followed by soft skills such as social interaction, computer literacy and etiquettes. They hoped that providing the youth with equal opportunities would at least help them tap into their hidden potential and improve their lives and of those around them.

What motivated them even further, as she explains, was not the recognition they received early on in their work but the zeal with which the unfortunate lived. It was fascinating to see and observe people who had nothing to look forward to in life live with the contentment and satisfaction of those who had everything they could dream of. A great example is Lata, a student of one of their care centers, who having gone through their training, has now managed to open her own parlor for other children in the vicinity. Geeta feels quite strongly about this and seems to think that her own life until now has been spent in a constant race towards accumulating greater wealth, power and status. However, the level of satisfaction she gains from the smiles of her children never ceases to amaze her and she regrets not having started her work earlier on.

When discussing the actual structure and start of *Ek Tara*, Geeta says that establishing themselves proved a non-trivial affair given the current state of our country and its attitude towards this class of society. While the government cannot sustain socio-economic development without the help of NGOs, it still makes it very difficult for them to function smoothly. However, the determined pair were not about to lose faith in the system and continued the uphill struggle to establish *Ek Tara*. Today, their foundation can boast of multiple care centers with a team of 15 teachers under its belt.

Ek Tara is a classic example of an NGO that has made a real difference in the lives of those in dire need of support. Its model does not mimic those of mainstream organizations looking to build a corporate profile under the social framework. Its success can be directly observed from the tangible differences made in the lives of children who are now able to converse in English, operate the computer with ease and can look forward to a life with more opportunities than they ever thought possible. Soon, *Ek Tara* will start vocational courses for the older individuals that will help them enter the job market with the confidence and zeal that their more fortunate peers possess. Potential tie-ups with larger NGOs are also being sought, which would help *Ek Tara* widen its reach without compromising on the quality it wishes to maintain.

Geeta proudly says, "I am proud of the developments that have taken place at *Ek Tara*, particularly the level of awareness and the dramatic improvements in the lives of the people we closely work with. Recognition by established larger organizations such as iCONGO has not only strengthened my views but also has motivated me to further develop our work to reach the farthest corners of society."

Ek Tara is not just about social change, but a story of an ordinary individual trying to make a difference. The USP of

Ek Tara is this - two friends coming together to give wings to a shared passion and follow its path to wherever it might lead. Few people have the courage and motivation to walk an unknown path and this is exactly what defines Geeta and Jaya.

BIOGRAPHER

Karan Puri, is Geeta Puri's son. He is a PhD researcher at the University of Bath in England and specializes in quantitative finance. He works part-time for a hedge fund in London.

Humility is the mother of all human values. It treats everyone equally, and gives us the dignity, integrity and courage to be ourselves.

— Jeroñinio

From an Accidental Corporate Career to a Planned Life in Social Work

Anu Aga

Anu Aga used to be superstitious about death. Like most people, she thought it happened to others. Whenever such unpleasant thoughts came to her mind, she would touch wood to keep death away. Sometimes, when she traveled with her husband, she even asked the car to be stopped, so that she could touch a tree. But today, she is no longer terrified of death. She says, "I know that even if I carry an entire forest with me, I cannot change my destiny."

Anu lost her husband Rohinton Aga in 1995 and her son Kurush in 1996. It took several months and a Vipassana retreat before she could come to terms with her sense of loss. Those weeks of anguish probably taught her not just to accept the inevitable, but also to find courage to change what is in her powers.

Leaving her personal grief behind, she concentrated on the task at hand – looking after the fortunes of Thermax, the engineering company established by her father, AS Bhathena, and nurtured by Rohinton. Earlier, following Rohinton's death, she had become the 'accidental' chairperson of the company, after the Board nominated her. From 1999 to 2002, she spearheaded the turnaround and growth of Thermax. Over the years, Anu proved to be a successful wealth creator.

Anu could attain success in the corporate world despite the fact that she had not been groomed to step into such a role. It is as the chief of Thermax that the world came to know her. And it wouldn't be wrong to say that it was from the Thermax persona her other selves emerged and took wings.

In 2004, Anu stepped down voluntarily to work in the social sector and in a planned succession, the Board selected her daughter, Meher, to take over the mantle of the chairperson.

Today, Anu's concerns are focused on the glaring disparities and divides of our society. She believes that the reigning economic order has to awaken its dormant humanity and find solutions to the problems of the wider community. She has guided her own company to form partnerships with the government and civil society to educate children from the deprived sections of society and help them open the doors of opportunity. Change, she feels, cannot happen in a society that fails to tap the creative energy of its women, who constitute half its population. As someone who has made her mark in a predominantly man's world, in her talks and lectures, she exhorts women to shed their internalised self images of dependency and limitation – a lesson she learnt during childhood.

Born in Mumbai in 1942, Anu was the third child in an upper middle class Parsee family. Though good at her studies, it was her two brothers who were expected to take over the family business. "The message I received from my parents was that my aim should be to get married and raise children," she says.

While her brothers and cousins were sent to English medium schools, her father, in a bid to bring some balance into the Parsee love for western education, sent her to a Gujarati-English medium school. Though today, she is convinced that there is no inherent superiority in the English language, Anu says at that age, the experience left her with a low self-worth. "Perhaps, my father thought it alright to experiment with his daughter," is how she interprets it today.

Anu has fond memories of attending the annual Social Service League camps during her graduation years at St. Xavier's College, Mumbai. Thanks to these camps, she came to work with Cheshire Homes and was in close contact with life on the margins. This exposure also resulted in Anu opting to study medical and psychiatric social work at the Tata Institute of Social Sciences (TISS). There, she topped her class both the years. She could have gone abroad, but "the messages drummed into me since childhood made me settle down for marriage." While sharing details of her growing up years with younger women and students, Anu often talks about the messages that girls receive at home regarding the stereotypical roles that they are expected to always play. These social expectations continue to dictate the course of their lives, she believes.

After marriage, she worked briefly – as a transactional analysis consultant to corporates, a volunteer for Mother Teresa's Home and a social worker at a school. However, during this phase, with two children to look after, she slipped into the comfortable and sedate life of a well-to-do housewife.

What could have been an uneventful life suddenly changed when her husband suffered a heart attack and subsequently, a stroke in 1984. Though doctors ruled out full recovery due to brain damage, Rohinton, with an indomitable will, recovered to a great extent. However, well-wishers suggested that Anu should join Thermax to support her husband professionally. She joined Thermax's human resources department. PM Kumar, who headed the division, helped her return to work life and later recommended that she succeed him.

Settling into the shoes of Rohinton Aga was no easy task for Anu. She says the biggest challenge "was to stop discounting myself and keep comparing myself with my husband to feel inadequate and small." Her daily meditation, self-deprecating sense of humor and the humbling realization that "our stay on this earth is short, our role dispensable and our impact inconsequential" helped her to stay calm, and also gave her the sagacity to ask for help. When her company's performance began to slide, she did not hesitate to hire an external consulting agency. Reconstituting the company board, she brought in independent directors and the promoters continued as non-executive members.

Even as she steered the company through its turnaround and revival of fortunes, Anu had been quietly preparing the ground for her future area of work. With the support of the board of directors, she established the Thermax Social Initiative Foundation (TSIF), to give a formal thrust to the company's community outreach initiatives. One percent of the company's profits was set aside for social causes (which has been subsequently raised to three percent).

Anu subscribes to the oft repeated purpose of a business enterprise – that it should add value, promote growth and create a profit. But, she has no patience with the facile statement that "the business of business is business" or the justification that a company's responsibilities to its stakeholders are fulfilled once it creates job opportunities and pays its taxes. Convinced that the "business of business is human welfare", she expects companies with their financial and managerial resources to reach out to the poor and the needy. For her, this is not an option but a necessity, considering the wide disparities that exist in India between urban and rural sections, the rich and the poor.

Remembering how her late son Kurush, troubled by the poverty and disparities of India, wanted "a part of our wealth to be used for charity", Anu began looking for a credible NGO to implement a structured community welfare programme. She met Shaheen Mistry, who ran Akanksha, an NGO in Mumbai. Impressed by Shaheen's passion and the good work done by her NGO in educating the children of Mumbai slums, Anu tied up with Akanksha, supporting its centers in Mumbai and later bringing it to Pune. Today, in its 23 centers in Pune, Akanksha brings together poor children, committed teachers, dedicated volunteers and available space to provide a few hours of creative learning.

However, the Akanksha Board was concerned about improving the academic standards of their children, and the limits of what was possible within their centers. Moreover, as many of the slums are frequently razed down in the city expansion or beautification drives, spelling uncertainty for the people living there, engaging children for longer periods became a big challenge.

The idea of adopting municipal schools came as an answer to this dilemma. The TSIF and Akanksha signed a 30-year MOU with the Pune Municipal Corporation (PMC), which runs 21 English medium schools. At present, there are four schools, which come under the MOU and two recent ones under a new partnership with the Pimpri Chinchwad Municipal Corporation. The PMC offers the school building and provides books, uniform and transport expenses for the children, wherever required. Akanksha takes care of the training and educational needs of the schools. TSIF finances the project and helps with the management. Every year, the two schools have been adding a class each. Thanks to the innovative and creative methods of teaching introduced by Akanksha, the children love coming to school and are eager to learn.

One of the schools, K C Thackeray Vidya Niketan, won the India Education Award among all government schools. The Award had been instituted by the Education Quality Foundation India. This year (2013), the first 10th Standard batch from this school achieved a 100% pass with 70% scoring first class and 22% distinction marks.

Anu is concerned about the looming demographic disaster if we do not educate, train and employ the large number of our young people. Cell phones are ringing in the new sounds of aspiration and colour television makes ground reality even starker for a large number of young Indians. Literacy, which was thought to be the panacea, is not helping either. Educationists have long been concerned by the fact that the pathetic levels of competence of our school children, especially those from government schools, have made people across India opt for private schools or tuitions. The latest findings of the Annual Status of Education Report (ASER) only underlines this sorry state of affairs.

There have been several responses created from people in different spheres of activity to address the need to improve the quality of our municipal and low income private schools. Teach for India (TFI) is one such movement, passionately supported by Anu. Modeled along a successful programme tried out in the USA and elsewhere, TFI recruits outstanding university graduates and young professionals under 35 years. These recruits, called Fellows, are given intensive residential training for five weeks and are placed in full-time teaching positions in under-resourced state and private schools for two years. In the long run, the program aims to create a powerful network of alumni, who, influenced by their experiences in the class room, will work towards bringing about systemic change in education.

Since its inception five years ago, TFI has recruited 1150 Fellows who teach in 200 schools impacting 23,000 children in Mumbai, Pune, Hyderabad, Chennai and New Delhi. TFI has paved the way for a working partnership between the municipal educational system, idealistic young people and some companies that are stepping forward to shoulder their share of social responsibility. Anu, who chairs the TFI Board, believes that only such partnerships have the ability to mobilize people at the grassroots level and get resources effectively allocated to revamp our moribund educational system and make it a catalyst for national change.

To give a sharper focus to its community outreach initiatives, the Thermax Foundation under Anu's leadership has decided to confine its efforts to the field of education for the poor and marginalized. Anu points out that in our country, there is no dearth of challenges or causes that well meaning organizations and socially conscious people can choose to work for – from health, child labour and malnutrition to energy security and public transport. Of course, these challenges are daunting. To name a few, political interference, bureaucratic lethargy, endemic corruption – these can weaken the resolve of even the most determined. However, Anu is confident that such partnerships will eventually replace the weary cynicism and energy-sapping confrontations that mark today's public discourse, and significantly improve the governance practices of our country.

As someone who strides industry and civil society, Anu is a passionate advocate for expanding the role of the corporate sector in maintaining the rich diversity and plural heritage of India. She set the tone, when she brought up the issue of Gujarat violence of 2002 to the center stage of industry dialogues. As the chairperson of the Confederation of Indian Industry (CII), western region, she visited the camps where the victims of violence had been put up. Moved by the atmosphere of fear and helplessness in the camps, and angered by the silence of the corporate sector, she raised her voice against the state's active collusion in fomenting sectarian strife in the country. A champion of diversity in national life, she feels that instead of "just tolerating differences, we have to actively applaud them."

Anu has never hesitated to ask for help, whenever she needed it. And she has also not shied away from reminding herself and others that every individual and every agency has to own up responsibility. While demanding account-ability from the government for the resources that are wasted every day due to corruption and mismanagement, she is convinced that business cannot succeed in a society that fails in providing its citizens the basic gifts of human life, such as health and learning. To make this happen, she demands that the industry stop being value neutral. She believes it has to take sides and in growing societies like ours, for justice and social equity, it will have to be an ally of the weak and the dispossessed.

BIOGRAPHER

A.M. Roshan heads corporate communications in Thermax. He has been with the company since 1996.

In most of history, change has been led by the few rather than the many. These few dared to be unreasonable, to embark on a difficult path and convinced the world to understand and adapt to a different thought process, for the benefit of all humanity.

– Jeroninio

The Gender Warrior

Geeta Chandran

From a very young age, circumstances made Geeta Chandran realize that she wanted to work for the upliftment of women. Her mother, Parvati, even though was a brilliant student, had to discontinue her studies, as her family could only afford to educate her brothers. When Parvati had Geeta, she ensured that Geeta remained an achiever. Seeing her mother's struggle, Geeta had realized very early that most women lived an unjust life.

Geeta's paternal grandmother Pati was one such woman. She lived a typical widow's life in Kerala, having a shaven head and wearing a coarse white saree. She was an affable person who nonetheless had to live according to the norms that accorded her a status several notches below everyone else in the family. Her age was respected; but her widowhood was seen as a blemish.

And then there was Swarna Saraswathi. She was Geeta's first dance *guru* from whom she had learned *bharatanatyam* at the tender age of five. Amazingly talented and a multi-tasking artist, Swarna's persona was swathed in a cloud of secrecy among other south Indian women of New Delhi. The women from south India whispered that she was from the *devadasi* community. That someone so able and diverse as her *guru* could be the object of silent derision impacted Geeta deeply.

This tensile determination to focus her life's work on gender equity and equality was sharpened during her years as an undergraduate student at Lady Shri Ram College (LSR) for Women, one of India's premier women's colleges. There, Geeta experienced the promise of potential. LSR was pure oxygen. Everything was possible! There were no ceilings.

Also, interactions with her intellectual peers at LSR, convinced her that for classical dance to reach out, it had to be demystified – it had to become more communicative and it had to speak to the youth. Geeta's entire life-work has been crafted on these invaluable precepts.

And this realization led her to the most important phase of her life, when she used her dance to do just that – dance for change. Her creative juices flowed around the issues that engaged her imagination the most: the plight of women, the injustices they encountered on a daily basis and also a crucial understanding of their creative potential.

And so these were the issues that Geeta brought to the fore through her dance. Using poems, novels, essays and scripts, she creatively choreographed a new and complex woman, who could find inner resilience and balance. She explored the gender issue through different lenses: women and war (*Her Voice*), women and the environment (*Imagining Peace*), women and stigma (*Kaikeyi*), against the horrific practice of female feticide (*Mythologies Retold*), women as the powerful creator (*She-Rahasyam and Shringara Vaibhavam*) and women as pioneers in charting their own futures (*Explorations*).

In *Unquiet Waters*, she gave new life to her friend and poet Lakshmi Kannan's words:

I take the shape
of the receptacle that holds me.
I take the contours of the earthen pitcher
tall, squat or lean.
I take the form of the bottle
Or the glass on the table.

I even take on the colors of the utensils
in which I dwell.
I am the waters that you can see through,
I am the liquid that is almost not there,
I am the one in receptacles
of various kinds, my shape not my own.
If you can but break the pitcher
and set me free;
if you can just break the pitcher
I would flow into the stream
gurgling, I'll catch the sun
in a jeweled glitter.
I'll run over the smooth rocks, swiftly,
to join my mother, the river
till we melt together
into the ocean of our being.

Much later, in an original poem created for her dance, she underlined the need for women to move to personhood.

I too want to be a Noun;
A NOUN!
Not just a mountain of Verbs.
Listening, Doing, Toiling
Cleaning, Cooking, Washing
Birthing, Mothering, Grand-mothering
Bleeding, Loving, Healing.
Just a mountain of Verbs!

I too want to be a Noun;
A NOUN!
Not just a pile of Adjectives
Obedient, Diligent, Patient
Intelligent, Hard-working,

Sexy, Affectionate, Home-maker
Caring, Darling, God-fearing.
Just a pile of Adjectives!
I too want to be a Noun.
Like HER. Equal. In every way.
I too want to be. Just BE!

But, the plight of women caught in pitiable circumstances over which they had no control moved her constantly. At the invitation of a prominent NGO *Apne Aap* working with women trafficking, Geeta visited their hovels in Kolkata. This led her to create her iconic dance on ugliness entitled 'Un-urth' where she presented the helplessness and angst of those women, who Geeta felt were trapped like mice.

She vividly remembers another incident that she encountered at the Bundi festival of dance. In Geeta's words, "At that district festival, which coincided with the main rural fair (Kartik Purnima Mela) in the area, there were over 30,000 people seated around the sprawling stage built on the banks of the quietly flowing Chambal River. Since this was entirely an audience of Hindi-speaking people, I had prepared a *bharatanatyam* program based on numbers from Surdas, Mirabai, etc. The crowd understood every word of the music and their eyes devoured every inflection in the dance.

"As the performance concluded, I left with my musicians cutting through the surging and milling people to the district collector's jeep that was to take us to Kota from where we were to board the train to New Delhi. As I was climbing into the vehicle, a group of young women surrounded me and squeezed my arm. A few of them were carrying their infants with them. One of them started sobbing.

"Alarmed, I asked what the matter was. They quickly made me understand that the young woman's husband was having an illicit affair with another woman in her village.

And she had been unable to speak out her hurt to him. She had been moved by my Surdas rendering of '*Mohe chhuo nahin, door raho*' where an angry Radha had chastized an errant Krishna for his wayward behavior. The dejected woman wanted to know if my expressions were from real experience.

"I spent several minutes talking to the group about their problems, the rights of women and the need to be vocal about their feelings. I said that they should create their own support system in the village and speak out against all injustices.

"Those few minutes with the women leading a life of struggle was an eye-opener. To this day, I wonder whether she had mustered enough guts to speak out to her spouse against his infidelity. I will never know. But I knew fully then that my art could move people into action. That at least was a beginning," she says.

Such innumerable encounters she had while traveling across India for performances consolidated her commitment to being fully dedicated to the cause of women. From the cradle to cremation, she tackled all aspects of gender-inequities through her creative dance choreographies.

In *Mythologies Retold*, she articulated contemporary concern against female feticide. The dichotomy in India's cultural practices tormented her. On the one hand, the *Devi* was celebrated and cherished, yet on the other hand her manifestation in the form of a girl-child was abruptly abandoned. The female fetus was not even given a chance to mature into a new born. In her recreation of mythology, she narrated a new story – how the construction of a new Devi temple had to be abandoned, as the chosen site uncovered buried fetuses. In one choreographic swoop, Geeta linked past practice to current shame.

In *Her Voice*, she probed tenets of Indian cultural perceptions of war and violence, and how they impacted collective psyche. In this iconic work, which brought *bharatanatyam* and puppetry together, Geeta, along with artistic collaborator Anurupa Roy, looked at the mythical *Kurukshetra* war from the *Mahabharata* epic through the eyes of its key female protagonist, *Draupadi* (who is said to be the cause of the war) and analyzed the pain and grief that she goes through during the war.

In Geeta's production, *Draupadi* accepts that she instigated the notion of revenge, but in a major turning point in her own understanding and evolution, rejects revenge since it only unleashes more pain and further misery. Rejecting the patriarchal vision of the war, one sees the horror of the war through *Draupadi's* eyes, who enumerates the horrible personal costs she bears as the deaths mount in the war. It is a dark presentation. *Draupadi* remains caught in the see-saw of avenge and revenge until she rejects the vicious cycle for a more conscious peace.

Geeta's production did not focus on the *Mahabharata* narrative. But it used *Draupadi*, representing a power-broker of the state, who urged war and examined her psychology when the costs of the war she inspired are most paid by her. The maturing of *Draupadi* in realizing the futility of war and conflict became the basis of *Her Voice*.

In a larger and broader perspective, *Her Voice* underlined a woman's impassioned plea to the world to see war and conflict through human misery-indicators and to try and create a more peaceful world.

Kaikeyi was different. In that production, Geeta approached the complex problem of women as victims of stigma. "Imagine, No girl child in the Indian sub-continent is ever named Kaikeyi," she shudders. Geeta analyzed the *Valmiki Ramayana* to create a character of Kaikeyi who was educated, accomplished and a princess trained in the art of war. Yet, when she asked for her due, she was the victim of terrible stigma and hate. This brought out so many contemporary problems of stigma which women face. Geeta's *Kaikeyi* invited the audience to reassess their stereotypical reactions and to engage with truths more meaningfully.

Another dance entitled *Explorations* was inspired by two paintings by the famous artist Arpana Caur. Geeta felt that Arpana's paintings caught the right dilemmas of the women's movement in India. On the one hand, women are still exploring new spaces that are slowly opening out to them, while on the other hand, they are reveling in the new-found spotlight. Both ends of the spectrum are valid. Both need the society's support and both need to be celebrated.

She shares her excitement and the philosophy behind her creation, "When I saw Arpana's paintings, I knew instantly that light will become a dance partner for the piece. Arpana's use of light sparked me to think of using light as a choreographic device. I had not done this before and was excited by the thought and its possibilities. Will it be feasible? Will it work? Such doubts did not enter my head at all. I was only fired by the creative possibilities. The vision of the choreography had been unveiled in my inner eye".

For a dancer, such moments are the most cherished. They inspire them to move ahead.

Later, at her studio, another exciting moment had her in its thrall when she was able to create two new *hastas* (hand-gestures) that captured the stereotypical situations of women. This happened with a conscious effort to deconstruct classical movements to articulate something different. This play, this ability to be unbound is what makes dance a tremendous creative art form.

Her choreography of *Explorations* was visualized in three sections. In the first, she portrayed a woman defined by the several barriers that demarcate her existence. Restricted spaces squeeze the very oxygen from her lungs! She plays stereotypical roles, is bound by custom and tradition and loses her individuality.

In the second section, the choreography presented a woman slowly stepping out of traditional boundaries and exploring changing identities. The ideas that she tried to capture were a woman's journey:

From Consent to Dissent
From Periphery to Centre
From Diffidence to Confidence
From Within to Without
From Without to Within
From Gender to Identity.

The last segment celebrated women's freedom to fly and liberty of choice. It celebrated a woman's 'personhood'.

This dance became very dear to her as an artist because its universality was amazing. In it, she captured the many journeys and struggles of her friends, relatives and students. She remembered her own journeys, conflicts and so many situations when one is plagued by doubts.

How often is it that women are forced to confront their inner voices and debate within their self on issues of identity? The issue of choice is a special burden for women. They have to transcend convention and societal expectations and step out of stereotypical contexts to establish their identities. But, then fiery ambition prods and one makes the choices that lead one to fulfillment. But, that journey is not easy. Women are caught in situations where they are confined by forces beyond their control. When they move out, it is in a zone of darkness. They have to chart their own course. If they fail, they are not accepted back. Their journeys have no destinations and no points of return. It is this fear that she always tried to capture in 'Explorations'.

Geeta says, "The dance celebrated women leaving their bundles of doubts behind and doing what they truly wanted - of their being linked with their inner voices and of reaching pinnacles of success which makes all the struggles and strife worth it."

Geeta went on to establish her own dance institute Natya Vriksha, where she mentors over 100 young women. They come to her not only to learn dance and its philosophy, but also valuable lessons that make life exciting to experience. Geeta enables them to find their spine – both the physical spine, as is used in classical dance, and the metaphorical spine that gives their personalities its dynamism. For centuries, women were supine, says Geeta, but today, a woman's spine helps her hold her head high and achieve her milestones with dignity. "In our spine is our freedom," concludes a smiling Geeta.

BIOGRAPHER

Rajiv Chandran is Geeta Chandran's husband and the National Information Officer, United Nations Information Centre for India and Bhutan.

We are all born as ordinary human beings. But, each of us has the power to rise above the mediocre and make ourselves extraordinary.

– Jeroninio

The Rhythm of Heart

Mallika Dutt

Mallika Dutt isn't easy to describe. She's a lawyer by training, who also happens to be an award-winning music video producer, and who also happens to be the founder and CEO of a global human rights organization. She's a 30-year-old veteran of the women's rights movement and an ardent devotee of the kind of pulp romance-novels that make most feminists blush. And while she has held court in the closed meeting rooms of the organizations ranging from the United Nations Organization to the World Economic Forum, Mallika is much more interested in what people are talking about in their own living rooms. In fact, she has dedicated her life to people's causes.

This is because Mallika believes that human rights aren't just the stuff of Special Rapporteurs or top-down declarations from political bodies. Human rights must translate into fundamental dignity, equality and justice that we all deserve to experience by virtue of being human. As Eleanor Roosevelt said, we should emerge, live and thrive in 'small places' – in our relationships, around dinner tables, at community centers, houses of worship and everywhere people gather to share ideas. Human rights must also be reflected in our popular culture, the media we consume and the art we make. And Mallika believes that *these* are the places where the real work happens – where a *culture* of human rights can take shape.

144

"I certainly feel that it's more likely for a middle-school student to play a human rights video game on Facebook than to pick up the United States Periodic Review on Human Rights report. That is exactly why pop culture has such potential for social change: it's inviting, accessible and fun. It reaches people where they are. It allows them to experiment with these ideas in a way that feels familiar and welcoming," opines Mallika.

It is this thinking that has helped Mallika to emerge as one of the most innovative, admired and effective leaders in cultural transformation today. She has made it her life's mission to bring the values of human rights and dignity out of ivory towers and policy papers into the lives and actions of real people. And with more than a decade's worth of award-winning music videos, video games and ad campaigns under her belt, Mallika is clearly on the right path.

Mallika's approach may be unorthodox, but she has evolved it as a product of decades of experience. And with human rights as a life-long passion, she's worn many hats through the years. As a young foreign undergraduate at Mount Holyoke College, in Massachusetts, United States. Mallika found herself – as early as in 1982 – working to establish the first 'International Network against Female Sexual Slavery and Forced Prostitution'. "I was 19-years-old and wandering around the red light districts in Mumbai and Kolkata trying to talk to sex workers as part of my senior thesis on their access to the legal system. I was so young and still had so much to learn. But, I had a burning fire in my belly," she says. Mallika quickly discovered that sex workers, women in trafficking and mail-order brides had little or no recourse to rights. It was then that she decided that a legal education would provide the skills that would help her address and amplify the human rights of those who needed them the most.

As a young law student in New York City, Mallika discovered another community with little ability to exercise its rights – that of battered South Asian women immigrants. While studying for the bar exam, she co-founded 'SAKHI for South Asian Women', where, as an organizer and an advocate, she trained volunteers, developed initiatives and advocated for law and public policy to challenge domestic violence in the community and to promote the rights of immigrant women.

After law school, Mallika worked as an associate at a tony white-shoe law firm. "By day, I was assisting in corporate litigation, which was an uncomfortable role for me to play. I couldn't see myself at all in the working world I inhabited from 9 am to 5 pm, but I followed my passion and my gut instincts when I was off the clock. I was quietly doing pro bono work related to immigration and reproductive rights on the side. It was a way for me to find a balance between the straitjacket and the unorthodox," she says. Using her connections in the legal world, Mallika established an extensive network of pro bono lawyers to represent battered women.

Since Mallika is an Indian immigrant in the United States, acting locally while thinking globally comes as second nature to her. While continuing her active volunteer role representing battered women at SAKHI, Mallika became associate director of Rutgers University's Centre for Women's Global Leadership. This step meant that she joined the global struggle for recognition of women's rights as human rights.

In 1996, after the UN World Conference on Women in Beijing, Mallika returned to India to serve as Program Officer for Human Rights at the Ford Foundation's New Delhi office. She spearheaded the foundation's work in police reform and forged partnerships among police, NGOs and civil society groups, and continued to support advocacy for marginalized communities.

Mallika began to bring her many worlds together during her tenure at Ford, but she was also beginning to feel frustrated in the traditional role of a career activist. "I was seeing the same faces at every meeting, policy brief and conference. The work that was happening in these spaces was critical, but the conversations were trapped in an echo chamber. I knew there had to be a better way," she says. Mallika began to search for a way to channelize these conversations into the mainstream and grab the attention of mass audiences. The question soon became not *if* she was going to do it, but *how.*

The more Mallika thought about it, the more convinced she became that media, art and popular culture were the right vehicles to amplify the voices of marginalized communities and express concern for human rights values in new ways for new audiences. This meant getting people to look at these issues in a radical way. What if we saw men not as perpetrators of domestic violence, but as allies in ending it? What if the stories we told about immigrants reflected not just their legal status, but their fundamental humanity? And what if the song we love to dance to had lyrics that empowered women to take control of their lives?

These were the questions that kept Mallika up at night and ultimately led her to a breakthrough. She dreamed up the idea of what would become *Mann ke Manjeere* (Rhythm of the Mind): a music video and album representative of women's dreams and aspirations. She had no money to speak of, and no rulebook to follow. What she did have was, perhaps, a hard-to-justify confidence and resolve that she would succeed.

Mallika soon found herself far from the familiar hallways of her desk job – that is, in the middle of a Rajasthani desert preparing to shoot a music video. She watched the lead performer, who was driving an enormous truck through potholed roads, perform with her heart in her throat and 50 women dancing in the back. "I was convinced she was going to veer off the road; she had never driven a truck before! I remember thinking, "What have I gotten myself into?" She negotiated permits and convinced the local authorities. She visited the major spiritual shrines in the area, asking for blessings and the success of the project. She could not have been farther from her comfort zone. She could not have been more terrified. She could not have been happier.

The matter of finding distributors for the album quickly overshadowed the exhilaration of making it. Meeting after meeting, blank stare after blank stare, Mallika began to feel that getting *Mann ke Manjeere* off the ground had become a hopeless endeavor. She had taken on a media culture in which women were more likely to be seen as objects of desire or disdain than sources of inspiration. In meeting after meeting, she was told that an album about women's empowerment would never sell. Mallika recalls, "I had more 'who the heck is Mallika Dutt' and 'what in the world does she think she's doing' moments than I care to remember!"

Though the industry boys' club thought she was crazy, Mallika persevered. Time and again, given her characteristically bullheaded refusal to take no for an answer, she insisted that her voice be heard. And finally, Mallika convinced Virgin Records to distribute the album. "My jaw dropped when we finally got through to Virgin. I couldn't believe it; we were really going to make this album," she adds.

With the support of a powerful company that was a household name, behind the project, *Mann ke Manjeere* took off. In what seemed like no time at all, the song reached the top ten on the Indian pop charts. And in a matter of six months, *Mann ke Manjeere* won the National Screen Award, was nominated for an MTV music award and created an unprecedented national dialogue about domestic violence and women's rights in India. The success of *Mann ke Manjeere* was positive proof that pop culture, art and media could reach audiences on a mass scale with a message of dignity, equality and justice.

Mallika used the momentum of this successful experiment to found Breakthrough, a global human rights organization that uses media and popular culture to inspire people to take bold action for dignity, equality and justice. "It was a natural decision for me to make. *Mann ke Manjeere* had succeeded beyond my wildest imagination and I knew we could keep pushing the envelope," she says.

Today, with an introduction from former President Bill Clinton at the opening plenary of the Clinton Global Initiative, UN Secretary General Ban Ki-moon as a global ambassador and a Cannes Lion among their achievements, Breakthrough's campaigns have brought human rights values alive for millions globally. Whether it's *Bell Bajao!* (Ring the Bell!), which calls on men and boys to bring domestic violence to a halt, or America 2049, the Facebook game for human rights, diversity, and democracy, Breakthrough has succeeded in making human rights real and relevant to newer and younger audiences more than ever before.

A scene from *Mann ke Manjeere* shows a truck as it barrels down a rock-strewn and uneven road. The driver fixes her stare on a desert landscape of improbably lush flora and fauna. She wears the quiet and beautiful confidence of a woman who is determined to blaze her own path. The road is rough and the vehicle lurches with each bump, but she looks fearless. She strengthens her gaze as her eyes meet the horizon. The future is unfolding before her. In many ways, this is the story of Mallika Dutt's journey to Breakthrough and to bringing human rights to the homes of millions around the world.

BIOGRAPHER

Katie McDonough is a writer living in Brooklyn, New York. She is currently an assistant editor at Salon.com, where she covers women, politics and culture.

No one can right every wrong. However, everyone can right some wrongs. And, if each of us does our share, in our own space and time, then together we can turn our world around.

– Jeroninio

A Life Dedicated to Music

Armando Gonsalves

"Hey, hey moga", sang Olavo Rodrigues, one fine evening, in Amersfoort, near Amsterdam, in 2011. This Goan singer, backed by a power-packed brass band, sang in his mother-tongue, Konkani, to a crowd comprising music enthusiasts from Germany, Holland and the rest of Europe. A roaring applause followed his performance, as the affable singer from faraway Goa quickly became the star of Amersfoort.

Never in his dreams had Olavo imagined of success in Holland. Because few years back, he was struggling with his career in Goa, and needed a much required boost. Things turned in his favor in Holland and in 2012, he once again became one of Goa's most sought-after singers. "That trip to Holland changed everything and I cherish it. I will always be grateful to Armando. He is still working out so many things for me," he says.

For most people involved in art and culture in Goa, Armando Gonsalves needs no introduction. "He is the real showman of Goa," says Olavo. "The effect of the publicity he gives to an artiste can last for an entire year," he adds. Supporting local artistes is just one of the many causes this bald man from Campal is known to champion for. From being a money-minded real-estate agent, whose sole aim in life was to get rich or die trying, to becoming a musical philanthropist – even if that meant losing money with every show – Armando's life has been an opera that's nowhere close to its finale.

This opera began in Panjim in the early 1980s at the Don Bosco High School. Like every city-boy, who passed through the portals of that hallowed institution, Armando's young mind too played host to the dreams and ambitions of success, wealth and fame. Father Cecil Noronha, the school's principal, must have been observing Armando, because when he graduated, Father Cecil drew him aside and said, "It's giving that gets you solace."

Back then, Armando, in his 20s, was confused. "I have no money," he wondered, "What solace can I get by giving?" In a world that promotes the unscrupulous accumulation of wealth, Father Cecil's advice was indeed strange. But, today, an accomplished person, Armando ponders over Father Cecil's words over a glass of plain tea. "You know", he says, "In life, I've learned an important lesson – the more I chased money, the further it ran away from me. The moment I stopped doing so, it started chasing me." He realized the depth of Father Cecil's words after 30 years.

Armando comes from a well-to-do business family in Panjim's posh Campal area. His father, Matias, trained in judicial service, was a businessman. His sister, Rita, is a lawyer. When Armando graduated in commerce in 1981, he embarked on life with a single-minded focus – to make as much money as possible, as quickly as possible. He never really had a job. He plunged straight into business, taking over his father's shop in Panjim's Latin quarter of Fontainhas. Soon, he realized that selling nuts and bolts in the 1980s was not a good idea and expanded the business to trading canned foods, paints and hardware.

Over the years, he became a successful businessman. It was Chicky Chocky, the restaurant he opened in Panjim in 1985, that he says, gave Goa its first pizza. "During the 1990 football world cup, I gave The *Navhind Times* its first color supplement," he adds. And in 2003, he lit up Panjim like never before. White lights shone from trees, homes and streets as Panjim decked up ahead of its first international film festival of India, which it now permanently hosts every year. He has also written prolifically in the Goan media, something he seeks to improve upon by writing a book that speaks about his two main interests, Jesus and Jazz.

The astute businessman credits his determination and commitment to his mother, Aduzinda. "From the time my sister and I entered school until we left college, my mother took a vow not to drink, and stuck steadfastly to it," he says. She also encouraged him to diversify and play the piano. "I used to complain about mosquitoes, in an attempt to evade piano practice," he laughs. "Then, my mother used to come armed with a hand-fan, and scared them away, compelling me to practice," he recollects.

For all the toughness and suaveness, Armando has essentially been a mama's boy. His conversations very often have a fond reference to his mother, who expired in March 2012. He continues to draw inspiration from her and dedicates a lot of his work to her memory. In the weeks following her demise, Armando worked on the Campal creek project, a civil society attempt to convert a dirty 'nullah' in St Inez into a tourist attraction. Armando's ability to convert tragedy into inspiration has always been innate.

Soon, after the turn of the millennium, he suffered his first major setback in the form of a separation. "While I tried to manage a financial crisis, my wife of many years moved out of our home with our kids," he says. Trying to find meaning, he sought divine intervention and was granted. "I gave my life to Jesus. It was a very difficult period. My concentration and eye for detail dropped," says Armando. Struggling to get out of it, he renovated his ancestral mansion in Campal. He then started hosting Panjim city's most memorable jazz gigs at his home. The performers were hosted at his mansion, where his mother provided hospitality and the home-cooked Goan food. "Music is binding; it brings people together," he says.

Just when he managed to settle his debts, and was looking forward to a fresh start, in 2005, Goa woke up to a screaming headline in the newspaper: 'Jazz enthusiast held for beating wife.' Armando, who always walked with his head held high, was charged with criminal intimidation and was arrested. "When the police asked me if I felt hurt that my wife slapped these charges against me, I told them, 'I trust my Lord completely, and he'll get me out of this,'" he says. Released on bail within few hours, and subsequently acquitted two years later, he believes the time spent in custody changed his life.

As he walked out of that jail, he emerged a new man. Since then, his accomplishments in the cultural field have become legendary in Goa. He gave a new lease of life to his trademark brand Heritage Jazz, which was founded a few years earlier. It is a commercial brand that unites three of the most important aspects of Goan life – home, heritage and music – and he is a formidable exponent of these. A fact he likes to play down is that he's an award-winning classical pianist, but has rarely performed in concerts he organizes, being more content as an organizer than an artiste, even though this is set to change since Armando has now decided that he will perform at concerts that honour Jesus, and of course concerts connected with his flagship brand *Konkani Rocks*.

Armando tried his best to get back on his feet, yet, there was a huge void within. From 2005 to 2008, he could not meet his children. This was yet another tragedy he was determined to convert into an opportunity. He hence launched two brands – *Konkani Rocks* and *Goa For Giving* in honor of his children Nihal and Zenisha, now both in their early teens, who are today, finally, on cordial terms with him, after several years of complete alienation and then lukewarm reception. Photographs of their childhood, along with his Karmaveer certificate, which he holds in high regard, adorn his office. Konkani Rocks is also a dedication to - in Armando's words – 'the person who stood thick and thin behind him during his difficult times, his girlfriend'.

Konkani Rocks and *Goa For Giving* are involved in a slew of socially relevant activities in and around Panjim. For instance, teaching music and art to slum children, orga-nizing workshops with established names like artist Unnati Singh and trumpeter Saskia Laroo, issuing scholarships, getting involved with education, and so on. Armando is on the governing council of the Sunshine School in Panjim. His house in Campal, which he likes to call 'the home of jazz in India', was done up in 2005, after his arrest. The mango trees that now dot its premises were planted then. "I was shaken. I had to do something," he says.

Uniquely, his slum activities are almost always undertaken with the help of foreign or non-Goan artistes and musicians. "They're usually easier to deal with. Our Goan musicians are usually demanding, while foreign artistes have come with us to the slums without any issue," he says. A cursory glance at his office reveals the presence of many paintings. "All this," he says, "is artwork done during the course of our workshops with underprivileged children from slums."

The Gonsalves Mansion bears testimony to the success of these workshops. In the spirit of giving, Armando has opened his home to music teachers and artistes to teach and hold exhibitions, free of cost – the only condition being that the trainers have to teach a certain percentage of children who cannot afford music tuition. Given the location, he could rent out the rooms to the music schools for a premium, but he isn't interested. "Don't even talk about that," he says.

In 2008, he launched the Jazz for Peace initiative in the aftermath of the terror attacks across India, an initiative that won him the Karmaveer Puraskaar and many admirers worldwide, including Jazz for Peace USA. The objective of those peace and harmony concerts was to unite communities. On December 7, 2008, a few days after the infamous Mumbai carnage, people from all walks of life lit candles near the Gonsalves Mansion in memory of those killed. Viennese guitarist Harri Stojka and Dutch trumpeter Saskia Laroo performed to the packed audience assembled on a cordoned-off road near the mansion. "That night, I spent over ₹ 2 lakhs," he says. Was he disappointed? "Not at all. I see it as my way of helping the community, and God guided me to do so," he adds.

He followed it up with three large-scale worship concerts in Goa Velha, Margao and Panjim. He says, "A spiritual awakening is an important part of our mission." These concerts, usually massive productions that attract thousands, are always thrown open to the public for free.

While *Goa For Giving* is largely Armando's charity arm, his other brand, *Konkani Rocks,* is his cultural initiative – an attempt to take his mother-tongue to the world. "Konkani music can be just as popular as Latin music if marketed properly," he argues. He tested the waters in 2010, when he executed the impossible – bringing Goa's most famous musician Remo Fernandes and the state's Edith Piaf-esque cultural icon, Lorna Cordeiro, together on the same stage, to a full house that comprised of mostly urban Panjimites. The concert was a roaring success, and though the heavens opened during the show, not a single soul left the venue.

The show was scheduled on August 20, 2010 – the World Goa Day, which was founded by Rene Baretto in

2000. "It is celebrated all over the Goan world, even in Karachi," Baretto says. "We tried to get our Goans to join us, but in vain. In 2010, Armando agreed to organize World Goa Day celebrations in Goa. Armando helped us make it known in Goa and the world over," he adds. So, a decade after it was founded, World Goa Day finally made it big.

His belief in his mother-tongue reinforced, Armando used his good offices with the prestigious Amersfoort jazz festival and led a contingent of Goan musicians there in 2011. The group included Olavo Rodrigues and Bollywood's legendary Monsorate Brothers, who he united especially for the occasion. A year later, Olavo had this to say: "Armando had complete faith in me, that I would rock Europe. And I proved it to him."

This writer shared a room with Olavo in Amersfoort, and observed from close quarters how much Armando's faith meant to him. And Olavo, like a true professional, left no stone unturned to completely captivate his Dutch audience, in the process adding a Dutch song to his repertoire. *Konkani Rocks Europe*, as the tour was called, was partly funded by Armando.

After its overwhelming success, he attempted to take the Konkani revolution to the next level. A repeat of the Amersfoort show was held in Panjim. Due to a technical snag, the show was moved from the Gonsalves Mansion to the banks of River Mandovi. Despite a heavy bout of rain, the show took off well. Along with the established names that sang in Amersfoort, the show also gave a platform to younger Goan musicians who needed a professional boost.

Armando gradually started getting more involved in his new projects, and his passion for the real estate business died. In 2006, Chicky Chocky was shut down, but Armando doesn't rule out re-opening it, and if he does, he says it'll be a tribute to his mother's cookbook. Today, he negotiates and brings warring factions together – yes, even husband and wife. More than a little ironic? "Not quite," he says, adding, "If you're part of the problem, you usually cannot solve it." While he does strike a real estate deal or two once in a while, he doesn't chase them like he did during the 1990s. He retains his temperamental nature though, and is still rather hot-tempered.

Armando has no intention of resting on his laurels. The free concerts appear to be on the decline of late. "There is no point continuing doing this – making losses all the time," he says, adding, "It would be prudent to ticket them, thus creating wealth for the people who need it." But, his dedication to the World Goa Day continues. A mega concert on August 19 every year is in the pipeline, with the usual array of Goan stars as performers.

Besides mission Konkani, his plans include initiating a kitchen garden revolution in Goa, and establishing a sister city connection between Panjim and Amersfoort in the Netherlands, both of which are similar in many ways. Plans are also afoot to start a brass instrument school in Panjim (brass bands being an integral part of Goa's musical heritage). Meanwhile, his pet project at the time was the renovation of the Campal Creek. Various initiatives have been unleashed in connection with the Campal Creek, with children's programs, boat rides, zumba dancing and other activities having been organized on the banks of the Creek, thus bringing in huge publicity to the project which even got the attention of the Honorable Chief Minister of Goa Shri Manohar Parrikar, who went on a boat ride in the Creek with Armando so as to get a first-hand view of the problems.

As part of his mission, he has assembled architects, town planners and other like-minded individuals from the area, all with a single mission – to convert the 'nullah', which is presently in a deplorable state, into a world-class tourist attraction. So determined is he to see this dream being realized that he told the government he'd reconstruct the bridge if required (it would cost around ₹ 2 crore). Of course, the government official politely declined the offer. But, why would he go to that extent? The mama's boy in him comes to the fore again. "This is my private dedication to my mother," he concludes.

Meanwhile, slowing down is the last thing on Armando's mind. After attempting to change Goa's cultural landscape, he, who now describes himself as a 'concept man', has taken his game to the intellectual level. "I want to bring about a paradigm shift in the way Goa thinks," he says.

BIOGRAPHER

Nigel Britto is a journalist based in Goa, who writes mainly on music and culture. He holds degrees in Computer Science and Law, and is interested in criminology, constitutional law, opera, western classical music and world history. Like every other Goan, he also enjoys playing music, and is partially trained in the art of classical guitar.

Our mind cannot be without fear and our head cannot be held high when we become slaves to materialistic values. Human values like dignity, humility, integrity and humanity are the real treasures.

– Jeroninio

For the Love of India

Arun Maira

May be it has something to do with his birth date. Or perhaps the generation he belongs to. Or probably the India he grew up in. Because, there is earnestness and passion in the way Arun Maira, 70, talks about India and Indians, which is both rare and infectious.

Born in Lahore on August 15, 1943 in an undivided India, Arun experienced life in both, pre and post-independent India. But as a corporate executive, a top-notch consultant and now working in the government, his work couldn't have been more contemporary. He had also worked in the US for some time and ever since his return in 2000, Arun has been talking about India finding its own genre of capitalism, rather than aping the US. "India cannot have the capitalism of free markets as we know it. Nor can it have the socialism or communism of the past. India needs a new idea of democratic capitalism," he says.

There are reasons why he thinks that way. "India is larger, more diverse and more complex," he says. "The economy must grow fast. But more importantly, it must grow inclusive. A country as diverse and with so many contradictions, can only move forward with an inclusive consensus-driven democracy," he says.

Is there a way to make this happen? If so, what could that path be? Over the last decade, Arun has researched, spoken, written and experimented, both inside and outside the government to find answers. And it is this thought leadership, more than his impressive 45 years of experience in corporate and consultancy areas, which sets him apart vis-à-vis many of his contemporaries.

Born into an entrepreneurial family, his initial few years in Lahore were comfortable, where his father had built up a flourishing engineering business. With a large bungalow, an expansive garden and a *buggy* to move around, his family had all the comforts that a well-to-do family enjoyed then.

But, that changed overnight. In 1947, the family fled Lahore and moved to India, leaving behind everything that they had to start from scratch as refugees. His father first found a job as the general manager of the Nawab of Rampur's engineering company before setting up a small engineering company in Uttar Pradesh with the refugee compensation packet he got from the government. Despite stretched finances, education was never compromised. And Maira soon earned himself a seat and a scholarship to study at the prestigious Lawrence School in Sanawar. It is here that he learnt his first lessons of what good leadership meant. "A prefect is given authority so that he can protect the weakest child from bullying, not to get favors for himself and his friends," he recalls.

Arun was in the school boxing team. Known as the 'scientific boxer', he used to win against stronger opponents by planning each fight well.

After school, he enrolled for an honors degree in physics at St. Stephen's College, New Delhi. However, his sole objective was to clear the Union Public Service Commission (UPSC) examination to join the government and serve the country. Nationalism was in the air and patriotic fervor swept the campuses. He remembers how in 1964, during the Chinese aggression, student unions in the University of Delhi decided to protest by shutting down colleges for a day. Arun, the president of his college union, refused to bow down. "We declared we will not close down," he recalls. His rationale – calling a bandh to protest against Chinese aggression was nothing but waste of a productive day. Instead, Indians must work extra hard to become a stronger nation; better prepared for such strikes. Initially they were booed – Stephanians were brandished as elitists who did not care for India – but soon people understood.

Arun's experiences in school and college taught him great lessons in leadership – most importantly that a good leader must 'choose' the battles and causes he wants to fight for.

There was, however, a hitch. Arun wanted to take the UPSC examination and serve the nation. But, he was under-age when he finished his masters. So, his principal suggested he appear for job interviews at private companies. A Stephanian graduate was then quite sought after. "If nothing, the interview call offered a two-way first-class ticket and an opportunity to see another city," Arun recalls. His first trip was to Kolkata. The interview was brief and casual and he was offered a cushy job and a luxurious lifestyle with a car, a flat and a club membership as perks. When he asked what his work-profile would be, he was told he would have to taste tea! He declined outright. "The best in St Stephens joined the Indian Administration Services and the Indian Foreign Services. Only those who could not, joined private companies then," he says.

He was then interviewed by the Tatas in Mumbai – a city he had not seen before – for the prestigious Tata Administrative Service, which recruited only one or two persons a year in those days. The interview was a breath of fresh air, spread over three days of long sessions. "They were neither trying to show off nor were they casual. They knew my passion was to serve the country," he says. They explained to him that building a strong industrial base, the dream of Jamsetji Tata, was also service to the country. "For the first time, I felt that even a private company could help build the nation and be respectable," he says.

Arun worked with the Tatas for almost three decades. He first worked as an executive assistant to Sumant Moolgaonkar, the legendary builder of Telco (now Tata Motors). When only 28-years-old, he was asked to substitute for the chief of the Pune factory, who had suffered a heart attack. Recognizing his strong people skills, he was also asked to build a system for developing Telco's human resources, keeping in mind their ambitious plans for expansion and for designing the company's own products to compete abroad. He was sent on difficult assignments like shaping Tata's pioneering projects in Singapore or troubleshooting the Tata joint venture in Malaysia in the 1970s, which was on the verge of shutting down. In two years, it turned around, outsold all international brands in Malaysia – at a time when the Indian industry and brands were unknown abroad – and made a profit.

In Malaysia, while turning around the Tata venture, Arun learned what drives great teams. The Tata team of Indian managers was competing with the best companies from Europe, the US and Japan. This was in the 1970s, when Indians hardly ventured abroad. As the Tata venture floundered, businessmen in Malaysia derided India and Indians as backward. They said that Tata's Indian managers had sought postings abroad merely to earn higher salaries in foreign currencies – opportunities which very few Indians had. On arriving in Malaysia, Arun voluntarily reduced his own salary, and returned the Mercedes car he was entitled to as the CEO. He made the point that he was not there for the money but to get a job done. The other Indian managers were surprised. Arun told them that what mattered to him was to earn respect for India and the capability of Indian managers. He asked the other Indian managers to reflect on what they cared for most. They said that apart from their families, they cared for the respect for their country the most. They too reduced their salaries. The shared aspiration of the Indian managers to prove that they were second to none made them fierce competitors and brought success. The Indian team was much smaller than the expatriate teams of other foreign companies. When Arun was ready to return to India, having put an Indian company ahead of the rest, the CEO of the largest Japanese truck company in Malaysia, with five times as many Japanese managers as Arun had Indians, said to him at his farewell that he had indeed proved that one Indian was equal to five Japanese!

But, destiny had something else in store for him. He had to leave all this at the age of 46, to move to the US to be closer to his daughter studying there who had a health problem and to his son who was going to college there too.

Leaving the Tatas and India to go to an unknown country and leaving a great job was difficult. He started afresh again in a new country, a new company, and a new profession – consulting. In the US, he took up his first consultancy job at Arthur D Little. And then there was no looking back. He was doing well – being sought after both by his employer as well as clients.

But, somewhere along the way, as Arun helped companies manage change, deep inside he longed to work for India. In 1999, while based in the US, he initiated the scenario planning project for India with the support of Montek Ahluwalia, who was a member of the Planning Commission then. He brought together Indians from different walks of life – business, government and civil society – to discuss and articulate their vision of India 2010. For a country too focused on here-and-now issues, it helped shift the attention to more long-term issues. And with the first opportunity, he returned to India as the Chairman of The Boston Consulting Group (BCG) in 2000. With BCG, he worked closely with India Inc. to help them get better. But, he was also figuring out ways to use those same tools to help India get better. The man, who grew up wanting to serve the country, wanted to now paint on a bigger canvas. And maybe all these years, he had been preparing for it.

Working closely with the industry association Confederation of Indian Industry (CII), he kicked off many initiatives. He started the CII Leadership Summit to help evolve new standards of leadership for leaders across the industry and society. He also facilitated a high level Strategic Group, a voluntary initiative undertaken by many industry leaders, to foresee the opportunities for India in the changing global demographics – a young India and ageing rich countries. This led to the India Brand Equity Foundation which attempted to reposition India from a land of 'snake-charmers' and tourist attractions to a modern fast growing, emerging economy and a destination for global investments.

In India, Arun played a coaching role to leaders in industry, and also to younger partners in BCG. When a BCG partner, leading an organization project in a large Indian public sector organization, felt helpless about how he could motivate thousands of employees of the organization across the country to change their attitudes, he turned to Arun. Arun said, "You cannot change a hundred thousand people, or even ten persons, unless they want to change themselves. You have to show them the way they want to go, not try to beat each of them to change." Arun's definition of leadership is, "A leader is he or she who takes the first steps towards what he or she deeply cares about, in ways that others may wish to follow." That's what Arun had done in Malaysia, and it is the principle that guides him in the many situations he has found himself, where many must work together to do what appears to be very difficult. When young people wonder what they should do in life, or when they complain that things are not going their way, Arun asks them to shut their eyes and consider what they care about most, and what they would like to contribute to others. Then, he asks them to determine what must be the immediate steps they must take towards that cause, and then just get going.

Amid all this, it became very clear to him that both electoral democracy and free-market capitalism were facing challenges from within which had significant implications for both India and India Inc. It is on this journey of discovery, that Arun has spoken and written extensively about 21st century capitalism and the Indian democracy. He has penned five books: *The Accelerating Organization: Embracing the Human Face of Change*, when he was consulting in the US; and *Shaping the Future, Remaking India, Discordant Democrats and Transforming Capitalism* since returning to India. All of them are thought-provoking and deal with issues like transformation, capitalism, democracy and the future of India.

There are two important points that Arun has been pointing out through his writings. One, that both capitalism and democracy – as we know them today – will need to evolve to meet the needs and expectations of the 21st century world. Two, India will have to find its own path – emulating the US and envying China will not help.

Why? "Three important mega trends are shaping lives, politics and business in the 21st century world," he says.

One, with communism dead, there has been an arrogant, almost unquestioning wave of free-market capitalism across the world, including India. Global economic crisis, greed and popular mistrust have now put a question mark. Two, explosion of media, Internet and communication has enabled ideas and news to spread seamlessly. Three, there is an awakening of human rights across gender, class and castes with the civil society emerging as an important mediator, bargaining for people with the governments and businesses.

Amid all this, the government's role is shrinking in the democratic world even as corporations expand theirs. Combine it with the fact that governments are elected by and answerable to their people but corporations are accountable only to their shareholders and you see a democratic deficit that is growing rapidly. That's the deficit that civil society is filling today.

All this has serious implications. Institutions and rules of the past will not work for the future. Democracy has to become a lot more consensus driven. From 'Occupy Wall Street' wave to 'Anna Hazare' movement, both the Eastern and the Western democracies are realizing it. "Democratic governments must learn to listen to diverse voices and then be able to build consensus," he says.

It is the same for corporations too. Today, they have a broader role to perform in the society. "It is not just about shareholders – they need to cater to their stakeholders equally," he says. "And they too must equip themselves with the skills and tools to engage with all the stakeholders. This is especially true in a poor but democratic India where there is a greater need to build systems to serve societal needs than in the West. We have to find our solutions here," he says.

He had wanted to join the Indian government when he finished college, but, life took him elsewhere. Arun was invited by the Prime Minister of India to join the government in 2009, as a member of the Planning Commission. With an impressive corporate track record, Arun was hoping to bring the two worlds of capitalism and democracy together in his new stint and experiment with some of his 21st century ideas. On agenda was to set a long-term road map for an urbanized, industrialized and inclusive India and even to help re-shape the archaic bureaucratic Planning Commission.

The experience so far has been mixed. In a refreshingly new approach, the 12th Plan is being prepared with rich inputs and discussions with a very large set of stakeholders to make it more consensus-driven. But, the journey has been equally challenging. "Change is never easy. To get out of mental ruts and institutional silos is difficult. There is so much inertia inside the government. There must be more passion to change, for the sake of the people and the country. Fortunately, there are so many people outside the government willing to give their time and talent, without compensation, for the sake of the country," he says. With their help, he has presented plans for India with a difference, presented scenarios about what the future of the country could be if people worked together towards a vision of the country they want to create for themselves, and their grandchildren.

When Arun's grandson, Viren, then seven-years-old, visited New Delhi from New York where he lived, he was dismayed to see the poverty. He burst out in anguish, "What is the government doing? Why doesn't it do something for the people?" Arun explained to him that the Planning Commission was making a plan and showed Viren a copy of the previous plan. Viren's 'advice' was, "Dadaji, what is the use of writing a book. Do something!" Viren was giving his grandfather advice that the grandfather had been giving to young people all his life. Arun is concerned that young people aspire to 'have' something – often more luxury, or aspire to 'be' something – a celebrity of some sort. He tells them they must 'do' something that will improve the world for everyone.

So, what next? His reply is cryptic – "May God give me the courage to change the things I can. And the serenity to accept those things I cannot."

BIOGRAPHER

Malini Goyal is a New Delhi-based business journalist who has tracked India's liberalization journey and its changing socio-economic landscape for close to 20 years. She is currently a senior editor with The *Economic Times*.

Real humility is that which treats a minister, prince, priest, teacher, waiter and janitor with the same and equal respect.

– Jeroninio

Concocting Inspiration: A Life Dedicated to Others

Kumi Naidoo

Coming together is a beginning. Keeping together is progress. Working together is success.

– Henry Ford

"Can you handle spicy food?" he asks, as he adds the final touches to a variety of delicious dishes he's just knocked together. Curried eggs, potatoes and peas, kidney beans and lentil-dal – all ready to be relished. "We'll start with the soup while the basmati rice boils," he says. I feel thoroughly spoilt, as this man fills his modest home with aromas that sweet dreams are made of. He serves a 'Welcome-to-Amsterdam' dinner with warm hospitality and humility. I had no idea he was such a good cook – how is it that in the 20 years that I've known him, I've never eaten a meal cooked by him? Then and there, I realized that my friend, destined for greatness, as I know he is, approaches the seemingly simple task of cooking a meal with the same passion and commitment with which he has lived his life. Why is this so clear to me?

Kumi Naidoo's life is one of total dedication to a principled approach of dealing with social, political, economic, gender and environmental injustice. Unwaveringly, he gives and gives off his total self so that all of humanity can hope and never give up on the belief that a better future for all of us, and the generations to follow, is indeed possible.

170

To delve into a quick flashback – the year was 1992. Kumi is chairing the annual planning meeting of SACHED, the leading educational NGO where we both used to work. We were debating the future of our organization, as we were perilously placed at crossroads, saying goodbye to a repressive apartheid regime and envisioning a new freedom. Kumi stirred the pot, constantly pushing us to think out of the box – to stop navel-gazing, to see beyond the individual trees in our forest and to see all the forests! "An illiterate adult is an illiterate child first!" I exclaimed. "What a bold maiden speech," Kumi said. I am protected. I know I have a friend for life.

Have you tried eating a bay leaf, or chewed on a stick of cinnamon, or even worse, swallowed a teaspoon of turmeric? None of these taste good on their own. Placed in the hands of a master blender, however, we have a completely different outcome. The right combination of ingredients in the right hands can result in a symphony of taste and a kaleidoscope of flavors that nourish and satisfy one to the fullest. How well does Kumi know this? He has lived his life in a way that transcends individualized, piecemeal, disjointed, fragmented and isolated approaches. It is about the connectedness, the coming together, the joining of the dots, seeing the bigger picture and finding a way to make the sum of the parts greater than the whole. He is the master blender.

Kumi was only 19, volunteering as a live-in house father at a children's home, when he learned to cook. "It was the boys in the home who taught me everything about cooking," he explains, adding, "Their guidance and tutelage were inspiring and in the process we celebrated important values such as knowing that *you are never too old to learn* and that *we all have something of value to give to each other irrespective of our circumstances.*" Kumi shared his cooking skills with his younger sister. When asked a few years ago by a British journalist what he was proudest of in life, he said, "Teaching my little sister to cook." Today, she is the best cook in the family!

Picture this boy in 1980 in Durban, South Africa. His mother has just passed away tragically having committed suicide. Single-handedly, his father needed to find the means to raise four children. The school was not an inviting environment and the country was burning, as resistance to apartheid increased and the brutality of the regime intensified. By 1981, he had been expelled from school, beaten by the police and arrested. Surely, these were the ingredients for the production of a delinquent. The odds were completely stacked against him. Many would have simply fallen off the tracks. But, not Kumi. He tended to that pot. With resolve and determination, he turned his situation around. He volunteered at the home for boys, fought the oppressive apartheid system on all fronts, got reinstated into school, eventually earned a Rhodes Scholarship and completed his doctorate degree at Oxford University.

Back in South Africa in the early 1990s, Kumi was ready to take his life-work to another level. But, how were they going to change a prescript of the Freedom Charter, the liberation manifesto of Nelson Mandela's African National Congress and its allies – *The Doors of Learning Shall Be Open* – from mere words to action? He was in the front line, relentlessly working for the empowerment of the disenfranchised, poor and excluded. "Adult learning is a vehicle for liberation", was his constant refrain. Being action-oriented, he was able to translate mobilizing chants, slogans and what some said were clichés, into real, meaningful programs that brought significant transformation to people's lives. After all, he knew that just throwing the ingredients into the pot was not going to produce the masterpiece. He had to mix it all up and turn up the heat!

And then it was 1994 – the defining moment. Free at last! Free at last! Kumi was a key spokesperson for the Independent Elections Commission, one of the key people on national television bringing the news, commentary and results of the first democratic elections into homes. Then... they scattered. They were deployed to various stations, as we seriously and passionately took on the challenge of building a new democracy. Babies they were, at times, feeling like they had been thrown into the deep-end; at other times, reveling in previously confined and restricted spaces that finally widened, opened and became accessible. In this new field of play, Kumi consistently fought for a strong civil society movement to advance a participatory democracy and for resources to be mobilized and channeled for the development of all. For the very first time, they were truly part of the world.

Kumi became more and more active on the global stage. At home, it became clearer that while they had gained political freedom, economic freedom for the vast majority was nothing but a pipe-dream. The pots were empty and bringing food to the table was becoming an even greater struggle than the struggle against apartheid ever was. And a realization crept in that for genuine economic justice to prevail in South Africa, a fair global economic and trading system was critically necessary. Kumi's mantra (with reference to Lenny Naidu, Kumi's best friend, who surely would have written this story if he had not been killed by the apartheid forces) rings true now more than ever before: The biggest sacrifice we can make is not giving our lives to the struggle for justice and a better world by becoming martyred, however honorable this may be, but by giving *the rest of our lives!*

Mobilize on all fronts! Our future lies in our own hands and unless we are prepared to make the ultimate sacrifice by giving the *rest of our lives,* we cannot expect to see a better world! Think and act locally and globally! Clearly, real power had shifted to the global level. These beliefs took Kumi away from home into the leadership of Civicus, the international umbrella NGO body based in Washington DC. During the 2000s, Kumi totally devoted himself to global causes. We, his South African family and friends, rarely got to see him in the flesh.

He pops up in every corner of the world. Now, in New York pushing the United Nations to hold governments accountable to deliver on the Millennium Development Goals, then in Hong Kong working with civil society partners to secure a fair and just global trading system, and later in Harare, evading the security forces of Robert Mugabe, consulting with Zimbabwean civil society about how civil society should be supporting their struggle for democracy from the outside.

At times, he is flying to Geneva to address the UN Human Rights Council on the linkage between climate change and human rights. And at other times, he is back to Africa or in the Amazon, working with Greenpeace partners to fight against deforestation, or in India and Kenya for the World Social Forum. He was then at Paris pushing UNESCO to ensure that early childhood education and adult education be given its proper priority. Recently, he was in Beijing, meeting with the Vice Minister of Planning, who is also China's chief climate negotiator encouraging the Chinese government to support a fair, ambitious and legally binding climate treaty. He had also been to Indonesia, lobbying with local environmentalists to protect the Sumatran forests, which are being destroyed at an alarming rate contributing to climate change on the one hand and driving the Sumatran tiger and orangutan into extinction. Recently, he led a Greenpeace delegation in Jakarta in welcoming the Indonesian President and several members of his cabinet to the Greenpeace Ship, The Rainbow Warrior, where he declared his support for Greenpeace's efforts in Indonesia and globally. On another occasion, he spent Christmas in Ethiopia, to work for the release of two anti-poverty activists unjustly held by their government. Today, Daniel Bekele is the head of Human Rights Watch Africa and Netsanet Demissie is the African head of Amnesty International. He later was working with First Nations people in Canada to draw attention to the horrific exploitation of people and nature emanating from the Tar Sands industry. He also turned up in places, where he clearly would prefer not to be, such as at the World Economic Forum at Davos, as a minority voice pushing for companies and governments to embrace sustainability and to put people before profit.

And occasionally he is here. "Kumi is in Cape Town." This is whispered as a closely guarded secret, as we prepare a quiet nest for this busy man. It has to be kept under wraps, as some or the other organization will entice him into making a speech at their gatherings. When he walks into my home, in one of the most beautiful cities in the world, he cries out for sheer peace and calmness. "I am tired of hotels. I need to be in familiar spaces. I need to eat homemade food. I just need to rest. I am glad I can crash at your place bru (brother)!" the travel-weary soul announces as he walks through the door. But, the vagaries of modern technology find him wherever he goes. His phone does not stop ringing and it is not uncommon for more than one video conference to be convened from the family room until the late hours of the night, restarting in the early hours of the morning. The only pause is for meals. And even over dinner, the conversation frequently steers to a reflection on an action or ideas for the next intervention...

Kumi is at work wherever he goes.

In 2009, as part of a South African civil society initiative called 'Save Zimbabwe Now' and supported by eminent elders such as Archbishop-emeritus Desmond Tutu and Graca Machel, Kumi participated in a hunger strike. When he arrived in Cape Town, after thriving for 21 days on water only and a further 10 days on liquids, he was decimated and ragged. Skin and bone. No solids for 31 days is no joke! The process of returning to food to heal and re-nourish his battered body needed to be a gentle one. Nonetheless, he agreed to address a meeting of the South African NGO Coalition that very weekend. Fortunately, the meeting was being convened at a natural spa resort. Our trek and stay at the resort are etched in our memories forever as the image of Kumi's emaciated body being immersed in the hot springs is so different to the standard oratory stance we so frequently see him in. A camp fire talk over the traditional South African braai (barbeque) reverts to the inevitable reflection on an action or ideas for the next intervention...

Later in 2010, Kumi chose Cape Town to launch his book *Boiling Point*. Surrounded by his family, closest friends and colleagues, Kumi shone! This profound work, following the completion of his doctorate from Oxford University, captures the essential thoughts of this amazing man. The act of making this publication available via a free download speaks volumes about the kind of person Kumi is. While he had possibilities of publishing commercially, he wanted to ensure that people who endorsed his thinking, many of them grassroots activists in developing countries, would have easy access. Some have since commented about this book as being the only one which comes close to predicting the Arab Spring and the Occupy Movement. The opening words of this work reveal a highly sensitized individual who, regardless of the international stature he has reached in his life, is still a simple man in communion with all of humanity. He says:

"While writing this reflection on the role of ordinary men and women in working for justice in the world, I have been aware that the act of writing is a privilege. There are still hundreds of millions of people who cannot read or write. Those who are able to read and write may not have the luxury of time to capture their thinking on paper. Others live in repressive societies where the act of writing, especially where it opposes the views of those in power, can mean death."

My story, thus far reveals a man, who is preoccupied with making the connections. It is recognized that disparate, disjunctured and fractured thoughts and actions can so easily place us in denial – denial of the inter-connectedness of how the world really operates and unfolds. Unless we can see how we are co-joined, we will all be stuck in our own silos forever obsessed with our own individualized and narrow issues and agendas. This will get us nowhere, or at least not as far as we would like to be. We will fail to see that when a butterfly flutters its wings in Brazil, it causes a hurricane in China.

As with the secrets of good curry, we need to ensure that we give depth to the cooking style and acknowledge the complexity of combining a wide range of individual ingredients and spices. In the correct proportions, with the right timing and precision, we can produce a culinary delight that no words will ever be able to explain. Out of the individual parts that have no taste value when we start, we can produce an outcome that in its totality brings nothing but pleasure and titillation to our taste buds. But oh, how aware we must be of the other actions that are required? How often we need to stir and nurture that pot. We cannot be scared. We need to be bold and brave. How much love, passion and commitment do we need to put into that pot so that what emerges is not filled with mere physical items but, indeed, holds the spirit and soul of its creator within the vestiges of every mouthful?

Now, a youthful 48, Kumi serves as the executive director of Greenpeace International, an organization with close to three million contributing members, in excess of 20 million volunteers, cyber-activists and others, and 4,000 employees in more than 50 countries. They needed someone who was a bridge-builder and alliance-builder, someone who was committed enough to work 24x7 and someone who was not afraid to take risks. I maintain that he was brought into that position precisely because he is a master curry maker.

His post is not without controversy. On a day-to-day basis, he has to deal with challenges that can knock out a world champion boxer in the first second of the first round. Focus vs Parochialism; Insider vs Outsider; Planet vs People. Forging a vision and an identity for Greenpeace in these dynamic and fluid times is not easy, as it is similar to chasing an incessantly moving target and forever facing the race against time. Believing as he does that he is on this earth on 'borrowed time', he takes on every challenge with such verve, dedication, passion and commitment that one would swear every moment he has on earth is his last. You will not find Kumi burning the pot, as he carefully tackles the putting together of the dish in a systematic, considered and sane way, carefully solving each problem that comes his way.

Always the activist, today he does wild but carefully considered things, ranging from climbing the legs of oil rigs in the Arctic while being squirted with lethal high-pressure water guns; to entering radioactive spaces such as the devastating Fukushima nuclear disaster area, to following presidents into rest rooms at Davos to steal a silent moment to make a point. Former fellow South African activists, many of them now suited high-ranking politicians, corporates and bureaucrats, ask, 'when he is going to grow up', meaning when is he going to drive a BMW and live in the leafy wealthy northern suburbs of Johannesburg. These entice-ments hold no attraction for him, as he devotedly continues to be a thorn in the side and conscience of people, who once were soldiers for liberation and some of whom have now sadly become short-sighted, self-enriching opportun-ists, betraying the very ideals that they once struggled for. Harsh words, yes, but a true reflection of what Kumi has not become. He still cooks a mean curry.

When I last visited Kumi in Amsterdam in February 2012, he had just returned from the UK where his then 20-year-old daughter, Naomi, currently studies ethics, religion and philosophy at the University of London. Kumi tells of the beautiful bond that he has formed with his child and how he spends much of his time with her, cooking a variety of curries. These are stored in the freezer and, knowing how tough student life can be, especially when it comes to feeding oneself, she is able to savor the taste of her daddy's curry long after he has left on his next quest. Kumi, the father, who has now become his daughter's friend, lives out that which feeds the soul. The main ingredient, love, is omnipresent. Not surprisingly, it was Naomi, who convinced Kumi to take up the Greenpeace calling. As a woman of the 'now generation,' she saw her father fitting in perfectly in a relevant international organization that was not only about talking, but also about doing.

There is a shared belief that it is through together-ness and connectedness that we will find a solution to the planet's woes. The commitment Kumi has made to close the gap between North and South, rich and poor, green and black deserves to be supported. When he points out, from the high profile international stage that he now occupies, that the 'poor are the first to bear the most brutal impacts of climate change' and those with power listen, we all realize that this man understands the kind of leadership this world needs to take us to a place of hope. Surely, we all share a desire to live a life filled with possibilities for a greater and safer future for all of us. We all need someone like Kumi, who has and continues to speak truth to the powerful.

Kumi's work is unfinished and will remain so, as it is probably unfinishable in just one lifetime. As he continues to build an incredible legacy, he can be assured that those that he has inspired will continue. In acknowledgement of the inspiration he has been for people from humble begin-nings all over the world, I dedicate the words of Zenariah Barends, another of our close friends, to him:

> *My dream is a thread looped*
> *through the eye of a common needle,*
> *I imagine cool water, soft bread and sweet smelling flowers*
> *a shared wish, a hopeful vision*

BIOGRAPHER

Noel Daniels has worked in all levels of education and training provision in South Africa and across all sectors – business, non-profit and government. Currently, he is the co-owner and managing director of The Fundamentals Training Centre (FTC), a company that focuses on provision of leadership and management training to corporates, government and communities, both in South Africa and internationally. He is also the co-owner of e-Agency, a materials development and publishing consultancy and he is the chairperson of African Development Options, an NGO which focuses on poverty alleviation and job creation in South Africa.

There is great pride and power in being a teacher. Those who realize this are transformers and enlighteners, because they have the power to see, touch and change futures.

– Jeroninio

Actions Speak Louder Than Words

Venkat Pulla

It is not often that you meet a person who has such a natural way of making you feel calm and inspired. I never looked for anyone to inspire me, as I always thought that inspiration comes spontaneously and not exclusively from a particular person. I certainly did not expect it from someone whom I have known for at least ten years. This changed five years ago when I met Dr Venkat Pulla as his manager and colleague. Although I am a social worker by profession, I surprised myself how much I allowed other people's opinions impact my impression of this man. When I began to spend time with him, I realized the extent of Venkat's passion for human development, both professional and personal, which he promoted in a selfless manner. This energy and his pure noble motives were often misunderstood and maybe even distrusted by many colleagues.

Sadly, it is often seen that people are wary and distrusting of a man, who is extraordinarily generous, unable to hold grudges and who possesses a vast sense of peacefulness. I struggled with the incongruence between what I heard about Venkat from others and the man who I was getting to know. I felt embarrassed that I had allowed so many false opinions to color my own perception of this man prior to actually meeting him. *Unconditional positive regard* is an ideal which is more difficult to realize than I thought and I certainly learned much after meeting Venkat.

In time, as my interaction with Venkat increased, I began to understand that Venkat had a personal discipline, which provided him with resilience to resist negativity from other people. Instead of engaging in apologetic arguments to defend himself, he would bring a huge dish of Indian delights, which he used to prepare the night before and feed everyone. It was quite funny how such peaceful acts diminished the development of animosity. However, some people remained unchanged. I once asked Venkat how he continued working with these people. Venkat replied, "Everyone has their own burdens, even the ones who appear to be dangerous. Hate is a paralyzing energy, which can only be healed with love. If you can send love to such people, you also return their hate." It made sense and I never forgot the idea that by loving an adversary, you stop their hate. I see this code reflected in Venkat's life, as he continues to have more and more colleagues around the world, who enable him to do his work. Venkat is persistent, positive and infectious with his inspirational ideas which are hard to resist. Most of all, Venkat has a healthy sense of humor, which lightens up the difficulties he faces at work or in his pursuits.

Although an academic in social work, Venkat held frontline positions for the entire time that I knew him. He looked for challenges at work in more senior roles, but these were often refused to him based on the office politics. Venkat remained true to himself and held on to his vision of expanding strengths-based ideas beyond Brisbane and Australia and this, I believe, gave him purpose and meaning during the challenging times before he returned to academia. His patience was rewarded and so was my friendship with him. Friendship with a person like him is an everyday reward. One can never tell what he will utter and how he will say it – incredible things that may affect you instantly and make your life matter.

It was not long before Venkat and I became professional colleagues and close friends. I did not anticipate how this would inspire me to work alongside him on many ideas that he was already modestly putting in place. Despite the fact that his career as a social worker in the department for disabilities in Brisbane did not reflect his professional capabilities, Venkat managed to keep himself energized by acting on his personal, spiritual and professional goals, which gave him a much bigger direction. Venkat works on the principle of reciprocity, which is fuelled by his understanding of change as a factor to any positive development. Venkat's philosophy resonated with me and I was keen to join him in his determination to ignite international discussions and contemplations of strengths-based practice in order to support best activities in all human services and endeavors.

Venkat grew up and lived for many years in Hyderabad. He studied sciences, which did not enchant him for too long, got a communication and journalism degree and finally moved on to something that resonated with his being. He married his beautiful wife Nisha who he met at the Tata Institute of Social Sciences, Mumbai, where he completed his doctoral studies in social work. He then relocated to Australia in 1992.

I am unsure of many of Venkat's life events, because we don't talk about that. I can never assume to be his biographer. I leave it to him to share his personal story, which only he can tell. However, just by meeting him, I know that he has always had a desire and a drive to promote social justice and reawaken a positive flow of energy within individuals and societies. I was surprised when I first found out that besides his full-time employment, Venkat spent many evenings and even nights volunteering his time to projects and activities for promoting dialogue on societal development through strengths-based practice. What surprised me even more was how very few of his colleagues knew about these modest activities and achievements.

Venkat has his own narratives. On his journey of life – the central theme of which is to reach out to as many people as possible in the world – he relates to one and all – be it homeless people in Australia, pastoral workers in Barcelona, youth in Nepal, a bunch of enthusiastic kids on streets, presidents of different nations, senior bureaucrats, ministers or political party workers. He helps them with a solution – a focused approach, a strengths-based practice and a change-centered attitude – that works for them. Venkat has always been searching for people like him – those who cause and influence change in the right direction. Be it, starting a citizens movement in Hyderabad to look into the state of environment in 1985, after the shocking Bhopal gas tragedy, taking the role of a public awareness campaigner for two years through the Ashoka Fellowship to sensitize media and NGOs on issues as big as nuclear power plants, undertaking the first social study of the tribals of the Polavaram dam area or inspiring environment education in schools in India, a legacy that he brought to Australia.

With such a precedence behind him, his search began once again. In 2006, Venkat founded the Brisbane Institute of Strengths Based Practice (Inc) together with a few volunteers, who shared his vision of supporting approaches that promote resilience as opposed to dealing with deficits. The institute hosted their first International Conference in Venkat's birth city Hyderabad. The conference was titled *Strengths-Based Strategies 2006*. This event brought together a large number of professionals from around the world, who used this opportunity to share their knowledge and learn from others' experiences. Strong links were developed with Indian and international academia to support the Sri Lanka School of Social Work. A conference for Venkat is a strategy for getting the like-minded to come together, as many social change initiatives are immediately created in those countries as a result of people coming together.

Over the next two years, Venkat visited Malaysia and parts of Europe, searching for meaningful approaches to building resilience in refugees and those who continued to live in trauma caused by war of civil strife. Once again, this led to conference strategies – in 2008 organized in Penang in association with the Malaysian government and in 2009 in Dubrovnik, Croatia, attracting international crowds to the dialogue on *Coping and Resilience*. Activists and academics from former Yugoslavia took cue from this to promote and build resilience in their own citizens affected by the Balkan war in the 1990s. Invitations to return to Balkan followed, particularly from Bosnia and Herzegovina, because these were new recovery ideas introduced to the region. Venkat visited Sarajevo the following year and presented a number of lectures and held workshops on *the Strengths-Based Practice,* which built strong people-centered networks. Working collaboratively with the Acting President of Bosnia and Herzegovina, Zeljko Kosmic and the Head of *The Gardens of the Righteous Worldwide* (GARIWO), Dr Svetlana Broz, Venkat inspired colleagues in Sarajevo addressing concerns of social apathy.

Back home in Australia in 2010, 'hope-building' was added to the theme of the conferences that he pursued. It was during the *Coping, Resilience and Hope Building, Asia Pacific Regional Conference* that I personally saw for the first time Venkat's ability to organize an event and present dialogue. With help from his network of international speakers, he inspired a crowd of people sharing similar ideas. The conference presented new models for building resilience in a world, which seemed less predictable and it shared stories of survival, which inspired the audience, such as the personal story of courage by the Ethiopian Mr Tewodros Fekadu, author of *No One's Son* (2008). The entertainment was provided by *Soul Gypsy* – an Australian music group of the diaspora from former Yugoslavia – which enjoyed Venkat's support and encouragement. I left the event feeling inspired and with a new zest for engaging with global and social justice issues. I decided to join the Institute and work with Venkat on the next project in Sarajevo.

The coming together of Dr Svetlana Broz, late Marshal Tito's granddaughter, who also wrote a well-known book on Balkan atrocities in the 1990s, titled *Good People in an Evil Time* (2002), saw the emergence of new networks and support for people's rights. The historic Sarajevo Conversations, 2011 was just the beginning of dialogue between politicians, corporate world and well-meaning young people with a desire to make positive changes in transitional and developing countries. Bringing the diaspora back to every country for interaction and critical support is Venkat's mission.

Joining the Institute gave me a much deeper appreciation of Venkat's abilities as a persuasive negotiator, visionary and mentor. Venkat's vision continues to be the creation of as many spaces as possible for dialogue between politicians, academics, professionals, business people, students and youths, who believe that a positive social change can happen in all countries, especially those haunted by violent history and/or poverty. Venkat's concepts inspire new young leaders of such countries as much as the older political leaders, who wish to see change as well as those who would have the courage and support to develop better social conditions for their countries. Venkat as the leader of the Institute inspired all volunteers in Bosnia to make this happen and organized a conference *Sarajevo Conversations 2011, to* suggest that anyone with an interest in contributing towards better societies was welcome to participate.

What is the connection between aboriginal history of Australia and Yugoslavian social history? Nothing. But, September 16, 2011 saw Aunty Lorraine Peeters, most revered elder of the indigenous Australians, have a conversation with the Bosnians about war, trauma and torture and about the challenges that were still being faced by the aboriginal Australians and how she was addressing their healing. Venkat himself presented a topic on applying strengths-based approaches when dealing with transitional societies. He brought in a group of young leaders, who shared their experiences in uniting and reconciling Croatian, Serbian and Bosnian people hurt by the Balkan wars of the 1990s. As a result of these conversations, these young Bosnian leaders made plans for May 2012 to unite and continue these conversations together with young leaders from Israel to continue the inspiring work which was ignited by *Sarajevo Conversations 2011*. Venkat lights the fire that ignites strengths-based practice for societal development.

The success of the conference was noted by many international delegates, who were already planning to attend the next event. The decision to provisionally approve training in strengths-based practice in African location has been taken by the Institute as a result of increasing interest and motivated volunteers in South Africa who have participated in the Institute's conferences previously and have been diligently coming back to the Institute's conference themes year after year. However, to hold it in Kenya became a possibility due to both personal and strong professional connections with colleagues at the University of Nairobi. So, the Nairobi University is being provided the first opportunity and a memorandum has been more recently signed by Venkat and the head of the department of social work, Nairobi.

What could one say about those who create positive change by bringing people together in a dialogue? Futurists? Strategists? Positivists? Activists? Rebels? Venkat, the founder of the Brisbane Institute of Strengths-Based Practice Inc. and Impetus Global, has the energy for developing conversations around building positive societies and relationships through exchange of ideas. What Venkat says, he does. He gets around to getting it done. The intrinsic faith that he has in people is something I will always talk about. His humility is his strength. Venkat has manifested his vision by bringing together a number of events in three continents, of people that inspire him and others, who share the same ideas of social justice and social development based on strength-based approaches rather than violence.

In 2008, Venkat was presented India's *Most Prestigious Civilian Award for Social Work – Karmaveer Puraskaar* by Krishna Murthy, former Election Commissioner of India. This is a well-deserved award, which Venkat uses for ongoing promotion of strengths-based practices.

Venkat is a modest man and working alongside him for the last few years, I can say with confidence that Venkat follows the vision that he has for humanity. His inspirations that you see on his Facebook pages are MK Gandhi, Sai Baba, Mother Teresa, Indira Gandhi and Medha Patkar – diverse individuals, which in a way summarizes his respect for global spirituality. Venkat is driven by his own values. Whether he obtained these values through his personal, family or cultural experiences is unknown to me, but what is known is that Venkat wants to expose in others the blessings, which he himself experiences through the simplicity of being and staying mindful. Such state of being has the power and creativity to change everything and all for the better.

Venkat has worked with me for a long time; however, after many years of being a frontline practitioner, he moved onto becoming a lecturer at Charles Sturt University in February 2012. I am pleased to see Venkat returning to academia, as he will be a strong advocate and a mentor for the emerging social workers and human service practitioners of the future. Venkat will not only continue to be globally engaged in conversations on how to communicate and build relationships with each other in a strength-based way to achieve just, fair and strong societies, but also inspire young practitioners to build on their own values towards environment, humanity and society. Venkat has been a strong influence in my life, as I too made decisions to translate my beliefs and visions into actions. It is time for him now to do this within an academic setting in which I know he will excel.

When I listen to Venkat, the future seems bright. He said to me not long ago that social work is a field of study with great potential to inspire positive change in the world through peaceful but potent interventions. It takes energy and collaboration to begin discussing any idea aimed at improving our world. The results are rewarding and the energy is shared globally from India to Australia to Croatia and so on. Venkat's vision is simple. As mentioned earlier, it works on the principle of reciprocity, investing positive energy into projects, which will benefit not only oneself but also others – individuals and communities. This has been evident in his work so far, the conferences and connections which bring so many ideas together from all corners of the world. There is a following of these ideas and a sense of loyalty from people, who are keen to see them being realized. This is not about Venkat, rather about the 'spark' which he is willing to ignite again and again in order to inspire others. In turn, he is inspired himself.

BIOGRAPHER

Stefan Bakaj lives in Australia. He was the president of the alumni committee of the School of Social Work and Human Services, University of Queensland and continues to remain on the committee as part of the team organizing professional development opportunities for social workers. Stefan is a contributing author in Social Work and Welfare Practice (4th edition) by Ian O'Connor, Jill Willson and Deborah Sutterlund Setterlund (2002) and a co-editor of Papers in Strengths-Based Practice (2012). Stefan is a senior social worker in the Department of Communities in Queensland Government. He is also a treasurer for the Brisbane Institute of Strengths-Based Practice Inc.

A speaker at a B-school, once told his students that they should aspire to become great like Warren Buffett, who bought his first share at the age of 11. If buying his first share at the age of 11 makes Warren Buffett great, then we have thousands of stock brokers in Dalal Street who should be even greater for having bought their first share at the age of nine. However, this has not made them great. What makes Warren Buffett great is that he understands the value of wealth, lives an austere life and uses his wealth for the betterment of humanity.

– Jeroninio

Ek Kadam (One Humble Step at a Time)

Meera Sanyal

November 26, 2008. Terrorists struck an unprepared Mumbai. It was the very same night that Meera Sanyal, Chairperson of Royal Bank of Scotland India, was in New Delhi, receiving a citizen's award from iCONGO.

The bank, whose Indian headquarters were located right behind The Oberoi Hotel in Mumbai, was directly impacted that evening. Overseas visitors were trapped in the hotel. The staff were trapped in the office. Panic and terror had spread across the entire city.

On receiving news of the attack in New Delhi, Meera immediately put in motion the bank's disaster recovery emergency procedures. This included tracking down the bank's 2,500 employees in Mumbai, ensuring all overseas visitors were safe and making arrangements to service clients the following day.

In contrast to this calm and measured response, confusion reigned among the government authorities in Mumbai. They were taken by surprise and bewildered by the attack. They didn't know how many people were trapped in the Taj and Oberoi hotels, how many had been saved and did not even have access to the hotels' plans.

Three days after November 26, when the terrorists had been killed and the last one captured, the usual debates began. All over Mumbai, hoardings and bumper stickers proclaimed: "We will never forget 26/11". There was a feeling of collective brotherhood, but also of collective helplessness. Everyone said, "The middle-class must enter politics." But nobody stepped forward.

Save one.

"People like us tend to criticize and analyze, but do not participate in the political process," Meera told me when I asked her why she had decided to step away from her successful banking career to enter the turbulent world of politics. "Politics matters and in a country like India, it affects every aspect of our lives. Watching the television coverage of the terrible attacks on Mumbai, I decided that if I felt I could contribute to solutions, then I should roll up my sleeves and simply do so," she said.

I met Meera in January 2009. I found her at the same meetings I attended, at public spaces where Mumbaikars were struggling to find a new paradigm for politics and active citizenship. At these meetings, I used to wonder who the charming lady in the silk sarees was. I learned her name was Meera, and found that though we had never met, our families were friends. Her father, Admiral Gulab Hiranandani, was a person I had admired since I was a child. Meera possessed an unusual combination of magnetism, intelligence and integrity. Most of all, she had a different feeling towards India than most of our generation. Inspired by her father, a gallantry award-winning naval officer and member of Union Public Service Commission, she saw service to India not as a duty, but as an honor.

So, in March 2009, Meera decided to contest as an independent candidate from South Mumbai for the Lok Sabha elections of May 2009. The time, she felt, was right to stand against the populist and divisive politics that dominated India. There was a need for citizens to re-enter and reclaim the political space. Inspired by the liberal tradition of C. Rajagopalachari and Minoo Masani, she felt it was time to speak up against the narrow, non-liberal and parochial policies that were beginning to dominate our country. And no matter what the outcome, she felt it was time that someone took the first step – *Ek Kadam* – to make a beginning.

I offered to be her press secretary and manage the press and publicity. Other friends and citizen activists offered to be the campaign's 'think tank'. Over the course of the next two months, the team matured. We met once or twice a week at Meera's home at nights after work and on weekends. We were an all-volunteer force, drawn from various walks of life, driven by the desire to create change. We drew up an agenda to get Mumbai back on track.

Meera formally declared herself as a candidate on Friday, March 20, 2009. We had 40 days to campaign – in a constituency that had recently been de-limited, standing against two sitting Members of Parliament – Milind Deora of the Congress and Mohan Rawale of the Shiv Sena, plus 18 other candidates – was no small feat. It was a tough task indeed, and one that would demand intensive campaigning.

Meera captured the headlines immediately. Here was a fresh, new face; a citizen candidate; an eminent banker who was highly respected; a woman from Mumbai's world of business; and a campaigner with a real strategy to put Mumbai, and even India back on track. Her campaign began to help heal some of the painful wounds of 26/11.

My phone didn't stop ringing for weeks. We were punching way above our weight from the start. Our campaigning efforts clearly showed the vacuum that existed and the public hunger for honest and credible leadership.

A week later, Mallika Sarabhai from Ahmedabad announced that she, too, would stand as an independent candidate from her hometown. She was followed shortly thereafter by Captain Gopinath, founder of the low-cost carrier Deccan Airways, who announced his independent candidature from Bengaluru. It felt as if a movement had begun. The country and the media were riveted by these new developments.

Several volunteers began joining the campaign; students, senior citizens, teachers, lawyers, shopkeepers – all wanted to be a part of this movement for clean politics. The social media campaign on Facebook and Twitter took off in a grand manner, Indians across the country and abroad enthusiastically started supporting Meera's campaign.

Our learning curve was steep. We struggled to get the voters' lists, or even be allotted a symbol of our choice. Wanting to run a completely kosher campaign, we worked hard to comply with the election rules, the complex accounting forms and submissions. It soon became clear that the logistics of fighting an election in India were daunting. On the other hand, we were overwhelmed by the goodwill that Meera was receiving from both the media and from citizen's groups – this was the wind beneath our wings.

The press and the television coverage helped enormously in focusing on issues that needed to be addressed. We went to every citizen meeting, candidates' debate and media interview that we were invited to. Backed by a virtual team of young researchers, Meera had the inputs and data to present a reasoned point of view on issues that were important not just for Mumbai, but for all of India. Soon, she was being pitched against the party spokespersons of the leading political parties on prime time national television.

However, this was not merely a media campaign. Meera wanted to walk the streets of her city and learn about the concerns of its citizens. She did not believe in campaigning in fancy jeeps or by rath yatras. She decided to do a *pad yatra* – a campaign on foot through the length and breadth of South Mumbai to meet its citizens face-to-face.

Meera explained her idea clearly, "If I am to represent Mumbai, then I can only do so by understanding the issues of our chawls and slums, just as much as I understand the issues of banking and finance."

Of course, none of us had any idea as to how to go about this. But, help comes when needed. A former politician, who no longer bought the philosophy of the political party he had worked for all his life, offered to take us through the streets of Mumbai, and teach us the ropes of door-to-door campaigning. Just what we were looking for!

Fortune favored us regarding the election symbol too. When she was denied each one of the symbols she requested, Meera finally picked the ballebaz or batsman. The timing was fortuitous – the second season of the Indian Premier League tournament was about to begin and cricket fever was at its peak. We got creative: our young volunteers donned cricketers' garb including kneeguards and helmets and walked with us in the scorching April heat, asking people to 'bat for Meera'.

The connect with Mumbaikars was immediate. "How would you choose the best cricketers for the Indian cricket team?" Meera would ask. "Should you select someone because he is the son of a famous cricketer? Or because he can buy a place in the team?" "No!" the public would roar, "We want the best cricketers in our team." "Then we must ensure that the most important Indian team of all, our Parliament, also has the best players," Meera would say, and people would laugh in understanding and agreement.

The message that we were serious about walking the talk, spread swiftly. Local community workers, who knew the smallest gullies of South Bombay, joined the team. In no time, they took over the management of the *padyatras,* which became the cornerstone of our daily routine.

The *padyatra* campaign started at 6:30 am each day from a slum and finished there by 9:30 am. From 9:30 am to 12 noon, we walked through chawls and high-rise apartment blocks, followed by a brief break for lunch. In the afternoon, the campaign team re-grouped to take stock and share updates; we also gave media interviews either at the campaign office or in television studios.

In the evenings, the *padyatra* started again at 5 pm and continued until 7 pm. This was followed by the meet-the-candidate events organized by Area Local Management Committees or citizens groups like the Rotary Club until 9 pm. Then, we visited the homes of active citizens who had organized 'Water with Meera' sessions to answer questions and seek support.

We requested that only water be served at such sessions, as we didn't want any of our supporters to be out of pocket for the campaign. Besides, the Election Commission's campaign rules were so stringent that if anyone spent money on us, it would be accounted for under our campaign expense limit!

So, while we were working hard to stay within the Election Commission spending limit of ₹ 25 lakhs, rival candidates had larger-than-life-size images of themselves splashed across the city, and on the front pages of the newspapers.

We saw the city, and we saw the system. We began to understand what a heavy tax the poor pay for basic amenities: ₹ 2 to use the Sulabh Sauchalaya toilets, ₹ 5 for a bucket of water and bribes for essential things like gaining admission to a municipal school or for receiving a death certificate... the list was endless. It was especially tough for women who had to perform their morning ablutions on the rocks, sometimes in full view of men.

We also experienced and were amazed by the sense of community in the chawls and the slums and the warmth and hospitality with which we were welcomed. The homes were tiny, but the hearts of those who lived there were giant-sized. And everywhere was the presence of God – at every few steps was a small temple or mosque or church and often, just a tiny shrine with an image of Sai Baba, or Jesus Christ or Hanuman decorated with a small offering of flowers.

Everywhere Meera went, she asked not for votes but blessings. The over-arching image of her campaign in my mind is the number of elders across the slums we visited, who had placed their hands on her head in surprise and sometimes with tears in their eyes, as she bent to touch their feet.

People were surprised how freely we moved and went unmolested even in the toughest areas of Mumbai. In fact, at her first official citizens' debate, Meera was warned away from visiting the slums by one of her rival candidates. Then something suddenly changed. The fellow candidate was handed a citizen's charter in English to sign and struggled to decipher it; Meera quietly translated it for him. At the end of the meeting, touched by her decency, he came to her and shared his mobile number. "Go where you wish" he said, "no one will trouble you and if they do, call me."

By then, Meera's popularity had begun to worry the political establishment. Pressure was brought on her to stand down. Prominent bankers and leading industrialists – people whom she had served with on various corporate boards and whom she had regarded as friends – mounted a campaign 'to vote for the lesser evil'. By standing as an independent, they said, Meera had split the tolerant and secular vote and helped fundamentalist forces to prevail. It was a clever party line, which corporate Mumbai suddenly had begun to endorse.

Ten days before the election date, Prime Minister Manmohan Singh came to Mumbai. In a shocking television statement he said to Mumbaikars, "Don't vote for Independents, they are spoilers." The media went berserk asking for our reaction, as it was clear that this statement was directed against Meera, the only significant independent candidate standing in Mumbai.

I was furious, and ready to file a petition with the Election Commission against the Prime Minister – he, of all people, could not make such un-constitutional statements.

Meera responded with her usual grace to the television channels that besieged her. She said, "I greatly respect Dr Singh and as a citizen of India, he is entitled to his views. But, equally as a citizen of democratic India, I am entitled to stand for elections. And what we need from our politicians is more independent thought, not less."

April 30 was the voting day. The polling was well-organized, but the voting itself was faulty: many citizens could not find their names on the list and had to return home disappointed.

May 16 was the counting day. The counting began in a desultory fashion, with mixed votes for everyone. By 11 am, it had begun to follow a pattern: independents and others coming in early, and suddenly a huge rush of votes for the Congress. It became predictable, and by noon, as if on cue, the Congress Party's counting agents sitting next to me declared victory for their candidate, and left.

An hour later, so did I. While heading out, I ran into some other candidates. They could not believe the results. One of them, who had very strong grassroots support said he didn't believe the voting – his family had surely voted for him yet the voting from his home area showed they hadn't. Another could not believe he had not received even a single vote in many booths: "At least my election agents would have voted for me," he said. (Both have since filed a petition with the Election Commission, and the controversy over manipulation of the electronic voting machines erupted with fury in the following months – with an inconclusive outcome.)

We lost our deposit – Meera won just 10,157 votes. I know my mother and I both voted for her from our area, yet the electronic voting machine at our booth showed no votes. Our moment to be counted in the great Indian election had simply disappeared. I didn't count.

Neither did Meera nor so it seemed the establishment. In reality, of course, she had made a magnificent difference. She had inspired many ordinary citizens around the country to stand for elections, and that seed sowed by her has now become a movement that is gathering strength. It was witnessed most recently in the 2012 Mumbai local elections when many stepped forward to contest as independents for all the 227 wards. Only one independent candidate won, but it was a giant first step.

Meera will stand for the next election, and the next and the next. Meanwhile, she has taken over and revived the Indian Liberal Group – the original movement started by the feisty Minoo Masani of Mumbai. Building the intellectual base of such movements is vital – we must think, not just act – for this alone will give India an even and fair chance at development and social justice.

During 2012, Meera undertook a journey to the villages of India. Traveling by train and bus, she visited over 120 villages across 15 states, to experience the challenges faced by the poorest of women in tribal and rural areas.

"My *padyatra* during my 2009 campaign in Mumbai taught me some very powerful lessons. Politicians in India are so busy contesting for elections that they forget what it is they stand for. It is only when I saw and experienced the lives of those who I sought to represent, not just of Mumbaikars, but of women across our country, that I began to understand what needed to change and how to go about it. Mumbai was only the first step of a journey that I will continue for the rest of my life," says Meera.

Ek Kadam: only one humble step at a time, but the first one in a long journey. India will hear more from Meera in the future.

BIOGRAPHER

Manjeet Kripalani is the co-founder and executive director of Gateway House, a foreign policy think tank in Mumbai. Prior to this, she was the India bureau chief of *Business Week* magazine, based in Mumbai, for 14 years. During her extensive career in journalism (*Business Week, Worth* and *Forbes* magazines), she has won several awards, including the Gerald Loeb Award, the George Polk Award, Overseas Press Club and Daniel Pearl Awards. Kripalani was the 2006-07, Edward R Murrow Press Fellow at the Council on Foreign Relations, New York, which inspired her to found Gateway House.

She sits on the board of the International Centre for Journalists, the Overseas Press Club, and the Indian Liberal Group.

They can defame, corrupt, imprison, exile, harm or even kill us, but they cannot destroy our ideas. A people's collective ideology shall always prevail.

– Jeroninio

The Unlikely Hero

Javed Ahmad Tak

The first thing you notice about Javed Ahmad Tak is his smile. The way it plays at the corners of his mouth and breaks into a broad grin that lights up his eyes, it envelops you in its calm, comforting warmth. 'All is well', it seems to say. And it is, till you remember why the young man had not stood up to welcome you as you were shown into his room.

Javed, 38, exudes an easy charm that touches you instantly. It makes you forget that this wheelchair-bound youngster has known trauma in its rawest form. He has even battled despair to reach out to others more unfortunate than him, and is today a tireless crusader for those forgotten at the fringes of our world, simply because their abilities take longer to be discovered and tapped.

"Today, I consider myself blessed for what happened to me," says Javed of his journey from darkness to light. "It is only by becoming disabled that my vision of the world changed." As his mother brings in a snacks-laden tray and retreats in silence to the doorway, the pride on her face is unmistakable. Indeed, his is a story of courage and fortitude, and an indomitable will that has made him a hero for many in his native Kashmir, a land that has witnessed violence and tragedy in thousands of homes over two decades of conflict.

Born in a family of modest means in Bijbehara, a town in the district of Anantnag, in the Kashmir Valley in 1974, Javed grew up in a community of artisans, laborers and merchants, where children quickly learnt to fend for themselves and plod through a dozen years of indifferent schooling, giving little thought to the harsh living conditions where nothing could be taken for granted.

Javed's uneventful childhood was spent in the stunningly picturesque landscape of Anantnag, not very far from the capital city of Srinagar. Amid the company of family and close friends, he too unquestioningly followed the tenets of Islam and found in offering *Salat* (prayer offered by Muslims) the guidance he sought to become a responsible adult and a good human being. Keenly aware of his social responsibilities, Javed became a regular blood donor and was involved with community-based activities like anti-smoking campaign, eco-friendly campaign, integrated pulse polio immunization program and so on.

Things changed as Javed stood at the threshold of adulthood in the early 1990s and the violence in the state. It was a period of great turbulence in Jammu and Kashmir, with thousands of youth being swept by the waves of anger and agitation, and unprecedented anguish in a community broken by the loss of loved ones.

Guided by his loving family's desire that he, the youngest child, become a doctor and support them, Javed obediently put aside his own interest in the legal profession and joined the science stream, enrolling in the Kashmir University for a bachelors degree in science. At the age of 21, like his peers, he was trying to make sense of the violence around him and was struggling to maintain a constructive focus on his future. However, Javed's life took a devastating turn that changed his life completely.

Helping an aunt whose husband, suffering from cancer, had left for New Delhi for a medical check-up, Javed accompanied her and her son, his cousin, to their residence and decided to spend the night at their place. His cousin, affiliated to the then ruling party in J & K the National Conference, was targeted by militants for being a politician. Shortly after midnight on March 21, 1996, Javed woke up to the sound of strangers breaking into the house in an attempt to kidnap his cousin. In the ensuing melee and indiscriminate firing, Javed was shot at from close range.

It was a close shave. The extensive damage to his spinal cord, liver, kidney, pancreas, spleen and intestine required multiple surgeries. His right kidney, spleen, a part of the liver and intestine had to be removed. Miraculously, he survived, though the spinal injury confined him to the wheelchair.

Broken but alive, a devastated Javed spent a long time depressed over the dependent life that lay ahead. He was certified '*100 percent disabled*', which did nothing to boost his morale. Dr Ghulam Rasool Mir, a confident and bold orthopedic surgeon, hid nothing from his patient, explaining that even a scratch in the spinal cord takes years to heal. He simply advised him to have faith in life.

Another inspiring individual who came Javed's way was Dr Shafi Ladakhi, a specialist surgeon at SMHS Hospital, Srinagar. 'God helps those who help themselves' was Dr. Ladakhi's only and constant advice. Young Javed chose to believe rather than give up and took up the time-honored advice of these medical professionals he trusted.

Confined to his room facing the street, Javed heard children playing on the pavement outside his window. Their cheerful banter brought him comfort and their sunny disposition brought sunlight streaming into his heart and life. In a short space of time, the children started trickling into his bare life, crowding into his room, wide-eyed and curious. Javed would spend hours talking to them, opening up new horizons for their fertile minds to discover.

The results were miraculous. Javed's spirits started to surge and he saw that despite the cruel blow fate had inflicted on him, he still had a secure home, a loving family and most importantly, an education. The pain of those more disadvantaged than him touched him deeply. "I took my life in my own hands, forgot my accident, forgot the past and started to live, making the most of my present," he recalls. "Today, I can even forget what happened on that terrible night," he adds.

Javed recalls the exact moment when he broke out of his misery and took the crucial turn, an incident that changed his entire perspective on life. "I happened to laugh, something that had not happened for a very long time. What followed was an awkward silence, my puzzled family unsure of what had just happened. Suddenly, everyone looked at each other and joined in my laughter, expressing sheer happiness and relief. This created a dramatic change in my life. I started finding happiness in seeing my mother happy. It was a symbiotic relationship we shared, and it only served to create more happiness around us, moving away from the stress and depression with a real and deeper sense of hope. Although I had been bed-ridden since 1997, I started life afresh from my bed, providing free education to those who could not afford it. The poverty-stricken children who had brightened up my days now became my ardent students, as I coaxed them towards an education that had played a crucial role in making me the person I was," he says.

Feeling needed and productive changed the way Javed saw himself. He was fired by the zeal to contribute to making the world a better place, to be useful to society, and to tell the world that the disabled too have abilities – if only they get a chance. He became the champion of the silent, unseen thousands who do not get a chance to realize their potential simply because they cannot see, or hear, or move.

Teaching the bright young children also inspired Javed to become a student again. He enrolled in, and successfully completed, two distance learning certificate courses from Indira Gandhi National Open University (IGNOU) – one on human rights and another on computing.

With a fresh set of skills, greater confidence and a deeper understanding of dignity, or lack thereof, Javed was deeply saddened by the constant social stigma that the disabled faced, made worse by the lack of access to their fundamental rights, whether it be education, health or employment. Agitated by the blatant discrimination, he started writing to the National Human Rights Commission, and the state commissions.

One of the successful campaigns Javed launched was for lepers in Srinagar. He took up the matter with the government of J & K, demanding due attention towards the leprosy-affected people in the Leper Colony in Srinagar. The chairperson of the state human rights commission, taking cognizance of the complaint, directed the government to implement measures for their rehabilitation.

Even as Javed successfully drew attention to the plight of the disadvantaged at various forums, he continued to seek ways of improving his own knowledge and skills. A chance meeting with a young doctor at a blood donation camp opened a new chapter in his life. The doctor, a graduate in social work, introduced him to his field of study. Intellectual curiosity aroused, Javed sought more information and successfully gained admission in the newly introduced masters in social work at the Kashmir University in Srinagar.

Javed proved to be a diligent student, implementing his lessons on campus right away. Bringing together students with physical disabilities to pressurize the university's authorities to address their non-existent rights, Javed led the group from department to department, identifying like-minded peers and making new friends. It proved to be a defining experience for him personally.

"It was a great source of pleasure and an important phase of my life. It enabled me to create bonds for the first time. Experiencing life away from my family, I built new ties," he says. Their efforts paid off. The university placed ramps at the entrance of seven important buildings, including the hostels, administrative block and examination block. For the first time in the university's history, World Disability Day was celebrated on December 3, 2005. It has, since then been celebrated each year with the participation of intellectuals, policy-makers, members of civil society and lawyers.

Armed with a professional degree and a better understanding of the various aspects relating to social work, Javed renewed his commitment to the cause of the disabled with added strength and visibility. He sought moral support from various community leaders and those professing sensitivity to disability issues.

Recognizing the lacunae in the disability movement in J & K, Javed filed a Public Interest Litigation (PIL) in the Kashmir High Court, appealing for improvement in the miserable conditions of the physically and mentally challenged in J & K. It proved to be a successful move and a significant milestone in the nascent disability movement in the state. It forced the recruitment board to draft a policy for the implementation of horizontal reservation for the employment of the physically challenged, in contrast to the prevailing discriminatory procedures adopted. The enforcement of the act was monitored. Universities and other educational institutions, also largely indifferent to the challenges, disabilities and special needs of the students, were forced to follow suit. Organizing his activities formally into a registered organization, he invested the sum of ₹ 70,000 given to him by the state for his rehabilitation to establish Humanity Welfare Organization Helpline, an NGO working for the rights of persons with disabilities in J &K including those affected by militancy. A number of advocacy-related programs are organized in Kashmir under the aegis of this organization. "For poor people facing disability, life is very hard and miserable in my area. Disabled persons mostly depend on social security. There are no provisions for them to get employment and live with dignity. So, I started my life in my own way," he says.

Today, Javed also runs a school for children with disabilities, the *Zaiba Aapa Institute of Inclusive Education*. About 50 children with different disabilities like visual impairment, hearing/speech impairment, mental challenges and cerebral palsy are given general education as well as vocational trainings. Samanbal, a women's center located in Anantnag, provides education and computer literacy to girls from poor families, empowering them to be independent, productive members of their families. He also runs the *Helpline Book Bank* for poor, physically challenged and militancy-hit children.

Recognition and appreciation for his exemplary work has been coming in from several quarters over the years and comprise a veritable catalogue of national awards. The National Award for Welfare of Persons with Disabilities in 2004 was followed, in quick succession, by the Achievers Award by Rotary Club of Kashmir, the Tak Zainagiri Memorial Award for Welfare of Orphans of Kashmir in 2005, the J & K State Award for Empowerment and Upliftment of Disabled People, the NCPEDP – Shell Helen Keller Award for Employment of Disabled People, the District Youth Award by Nehru Yuva Kendra Sanghtan in 2007, the CNN-IBN Citizen Journalist Award, the Cavinkare Award for Eminence for empowering the disabled in 2008, the CNRI "Servant of the poor" Award – Helper of poor and the iCONGO Karmaveer Puraskaar 'Chakra for Excellence' in 2009.

A regular and vocal-participant at national-level workshops and conferences, Javed has been a resource person at workshops for primary teachers on how to deal with special children. He is a tireless advocate for the effective inclusion of disabled in the census, actively organizing and participating in programs ranging from round table discussions and seminars to rallies on the issue. To make rights more accessible, Javed has made efforts to translate the 'UN-Convention for Rights of Disabled People' into the Urdu language.

Drawing attention to the need for acceptance and recognition for their inherent potential and talents, Javed refuses to accept sympathy or favors in place of legal rights. "A sympathetic approach makes us more handicapped and victimized by social stigma," he rues. Determined to drive his point home at the highest levels, Javed led a delegation to meet the Vice President of India Shri Hamid Ansari, seeking a rights-based approach instead of the meager pension doled out today in the name of charity. The delegation also demanded satisfactory implementation of the recommendations made by the working group, headed by Shri Ansari, for the rehabilitation of victims of armed conflict.

Well-read and digital-savvy, Javed literally has the digital world at his finger-tips. A laptop and printer by his bedside are his gateway to the outside world, breaking the physical barriers that confine him to his room. He is inspired by greatness, especially by individuals who have pushed the bar constantly and won against themselves. "On May 25, 2001, Erik Weihenmayer became the only blind man in history to reach the summit of the world's highest peak – Mount Everest," he wrote recently, adding, "Eric's achievement is symbolic of the desire of blind people throughout the world to pursue their dreams and ambitions."

So, what does Javed the person do to unwind? He listens to music, plays video games and meets people. Writing is a developing interest, as the string of published articles to his name shows. Sharing, bringing people together, taking quick actions – this is what drives him to excellence. On reflection, Javed is grateful for what life has given him. "Despite my disability, I have found a place in the society at academic and professional levels. I have also been rewarded for my perseverance and social actions," he muses. Indeed, he sums up his message succinctly when he points out, "One should not think too much about one's own disabilities or sorrow. Everyone is capable of achieving everything in this world."

One has to just watch his shy smile break into a good-humored grin to know he's spot on there.

Biographer

Chetna Verma started her journey as a freelance writer in the year 2011. With a postgraduate diploma in journalism and masters in mass communication. Later, with the thought of applying the age old adage 'the power of pen' to her life, she started working in the development sector with a non-profit organization called Charkha Development Communication Network. In this short journey of two years with Charkha, she got the opportunity to work in far-flung areas of Kargil, Poonch and Bihar. Along with writing, her passion lies in theatre that inspires her at every step.

Everyone is waiting for someone to change the world. What if each of us decides to be that someone? This simple change in our mindset can make all the difference to our society.

– Jeroninio

A Compassionate Healer

Dr Chinkholal Thangsing

Right from his childhood, he knew there was more to his world than he could see. Surely, beyond those salubrious tall mountains that he saw every morning on his way to school, he knew deep inside there was another world. "I had a strong desire to explore what lay beyond those mountains," he says, vividly remembering his childhood spent in a dusty little hamlet in Lamka, Churachandpur, the largest district of Manipur in Northeast India.

Chinkholal Thangsing was an extremely curious child. He was always 'too big for his boots' – but in a positive sense. He'd always wanted to know more and made sure that he found the way to do so. He befriended his elders and tried to see the world through their eyes. He was enchanted by their tales of hunting expeditions and prodded them to tell him more. He has always known what he wanted.

So, at the age of 13, when this mild-mannered and soft-spoken child set his mind to be a bureaucrat, it was in all seriousness. In his mind, he painted a picture of himself heading a law enforcement agency. But, there was one thing that he had never even considered – becoming a doctor. It pained this sensitive child to see any kind of suffering and if he became a doctor, he knew that he would be a witness to those pains. Therefore, he made up his mind that he would be anything but a doctor.

Fate, as usual, had something else in store for him. In his own words, he sums it up: "My life has been a miracle.

I have been led by a strong but unseen power and it takes me places without me realizing it sometimes." During a surreal meeting with a prophetess who visited their home, she prophesied that he would become a healer. The lady told his family that he was ordained or chosen to be a doctor. Her words proved to be true. At the age of 17 years, he appeared for a medical entrance examination and cleared it in one go. Quite a thing to celebrate, as medical entrance exams are seldom cracked in one attempt. He became a doctor, albeit a reluctant one until he realized that it was tremendously fulfilling to be able to lessen the pain of others, comfort those who suffer and give people hope. This commitment was further strengthened as he held his younger brother, who was dying, in his arms and he felt his brother's pulse till it faded away. It was then on that fateful day that a strong desire to ease people's sufferings and pain lodged itself in his mind. Today, those who know Chinkholal say he is the face of compassion. To many, including the smiling group of children under his care at his foundation, he is the messiah or God-sent Samaritan who can change their fate.

Chinkholal was born on August 6, 1961 in Mongon village, which his grandfather founded. The village is a two-day trek from Lamka town, the district headquarters of Churachandpur, which is one of the seven districts of Manipur. In Churachandpur, agriculture was the chief occupation. His parents, who shifted to Lamka when he was three-years old, did not depend on agriculture. However, like most people in the hills, they had a *jhum* cultivation wherein they grew rice and vegetables for daily consumption and occasionally went there to tend the vegetation. Even little Chinkholal would sometimes accompany his maternal grandparents to the *jhum* field and imitate the elders. Watching them, he learned to plough, sow seeds, weed, harvest and carry the produce of the field home. Sometimes, the little boy would stuff the greens in a small cane basket carried on his head with the support of a belt and surprise his mother in the kitchen with the fresh produce.

His father, a quiet man magnified with intelligence and wit, joined the Indian army, where he captained the football team of the battalion but was later forced to take medical retirement after a hip dislocation. He spent over eight years moving from one army hospital to another until he finally abandoned the Spartan life and became a teacher. Hungry for knowledge, his father enrolled in a night college and graduated and later, studied law. Senior Thangsing, however, was far-sighted and realized that he must educate all his seven children in a good English-medium private school. That's how the family left their village and started afresh in Lamka town, a more prosperous place.

Chinkholal, the eldest of the seven, showed early signs of being a leader. He led his siblings to school and walked the two-kilometer stretch daily. Sometimes, he carried his younger sisters by turns when they were too tired to walk. Unlike most children of his age, who shunned school, Chinkholal was unusual. He loved going to school and never wanted to miss a day. "I enjoyed the classroom, the breaks, interacting and playing with friends, sharing and swapping stories, jokes and playing practical pranks," he recalls. So, it became a common practice at home that whenever he was cranky, his parents immediately warned him that he will not be allowed to go to school and that's when he mended his ways and behaved. By his own admission, he was never the studious kind, but loved everything in the school. He proved to be an outstanding student and excelled in many extra-curricular activities. Even though he is soft-spoken and not overtly a fast talker, he was a good debater who knew how to put his point across and wax eloquent on any random subject with the help of his logical reasoning power. He took interest in sports and played badminton, volleyball, football and cricket. At one time, he even nurtured a dream to be a footballer. Perhaps, that's a streak, which rubbed off on him from his footballer father. Now, he keeps that passion alive by organizing football tournaments. These days, you will find him punching away the keys of his Blackberry engrossed in Brickbreaker, a game he indulges in as a stress-buster.

According to those who knew him in his younger days, he had many loving and unusual traits. He was always drawn to elders and not to his peers. He did not have many friends his age but chose to be among elders; he would listen to their discussions with rapt attention.

Being the eldest, he also showed a great sense of responsibility early in life. He soon became popular in his school for his organizational skills. He was the class monitor in junior school and a class representative in his college. He took delight in organizing events and meetings in school and college. In college, he was a part of various event committees and held several posts including secretary of the student union as well as president of the medical students body. He juggled his studies and had time to form a student political party and ran a student's journal and edited college newsletters. He headed student associations and was also the student president for his tribe for three northeastern states of India at the age of 16.

When most of his peers were struggling to clear their high school board exams, Chinkholal cleared his pre-medical entrance and was selected to go to a medical school. His father told him that since he had cleared the entrance, he might as well join. But, he did make it clear that it was all up to Chinkholal to make that big decision. "So, I thought for a while and decided that I should at least go and see the college," says Chinkholal casually.

Life wasn't without its share of hardships and challenges. For the Thangsings, raising seven children was not easy. "I recall it was a tough task to allocate even ₹ 90 for my hostel fees during my medical college days," says Chinkholal. However, his father was proud of the fact that his eldest son was in a medical college and overlooked the financial problems, viewing them as part of a temporary phase in life. He visited his son once in a while. One such visit turned unforgettable and that memory will always remain etched in Chinkholal's mind. He recalls that his father, after running his fingers over his trouser pocket, pulled out a crumpled two-rupee note and handed it over to him. Chinkholal was well aware that his father did not even have enough cash in his pocket to take a bus back home. This recollection of his father's sacrifice moistens his eyes even to this day. His father passed away six years ago and Chinkholal says it is his father who inspires him each day. "He is my hero, my guide and my pillar of strength," he says.

Chinkholal's stint in New Delhi did not start immediately after his postgraduate training in Family Medicine from the Christian Academy of Medical Sciences. He served in Selmat Christian Hospital and Research Centre in Lamka. It was during this time that he established the first HIV clinic and home-based AIDS care program in Manipur in 1993. The work in HIV care in Manipur was particularly challenging. Due to Manipur's proximity with the golden triangle and porous border, drugs came in almost as easily as smuggled cheap Chinese goods. There was a high prevalence of HIV and the community realized the need for intervention and awareness.

In 1997, he moved to New Delhi where he worked as a director at a medical center of a private firm and he was often engaged in providing AIDS care, undertaking home visits and being a volunteer from morning to evening. That period was an eye-opener for him. Back in those days, AIDS was an alien term and patients were treated like outcasts. He saw patients being shown the door, thrown out of hospitals and even at the AIDS care homes, where he worked, patients were being asked to move out of localities. "I have watched them die even as they longed to live. In their eyes, I saw their lust for life and a hopeless desire to live and be accepted," he says. And it was these ugly faces of stigma and discrimination that strengthened his conviction to fight for what was due, and what was right for those who suffered. "They are children of the lesser God," he adds.

So, while in New Delhi, he helped set up the first AIDS care home in 1998. The care home, named Michael's Care Home, was dedicated to one of the senior staff of the Catholic Relief Services who died of AIDS. The initial days were far from difficult. Once people became aware that the homes were for AIDS patients, they were shunted out of localities and often forced to close the operation. They moved from place to place till they finally settled in south Delhi. Within months, word-of-mouth spread like wildfire and the new AIDS Care Center was making news everywhere in the city as well as nationally. It served as an oasis, filled with love and compassion for the dying. "I vividly remember having to run from pillar to post, one locality to another, to find a space to operate our care unit to treat AIDS patients. The effort to secure a space was frustrating, as most who willingly rented out buildings would soon change their mind and breach contracts," he laments yet with a smile. And eventually, when they found a willing landlord, it was the local people who objected and even resorted to cutting off electricity and water supply. Anyway, word spread about the good work that this 'man like the smiling Buddha' was doing. Visitors queued up to meet him. All and sundry, including the capital's celebrity circuit, came to see him. Later, it was Hollywood star Richard Gere, who after hearing of 'this doctor' had gifted him a Yamaha motorbike. The bike came handy for Chinkholal, who used it extensively to the many nooks and corners of the city for home visits. Today, that bike is lovingly preserved in the garage of his swanky home in Gurgaon. He is still possessive about it and promises to never part with it. After all, it has sentimental value that reminds him of those days.

By his own admission, Chinkholal never had to scout around for jobs or suitable openings. Everything just seemed to fall in place for him, as if guided by that unseen hand he often spoke about. So, whether it was his stint as Chief of the Asia Pacific Bureau of the AIDS Healthcare Foundation, USA's largest non-profit AIDS organization, or later, as the Chief of International Affairs, Access Quality International based in Thailand, these opportunities all came along without him even having the slightest hint that the positions were gunning for him. "By God's grace, getting a job was never really a challenge. I do not recall ever applying for a job. I was mostly invited or offered," he says. And wherever he was, Chinkholal always and immediately proved to be an outstanding performer, hardworking and disciplined. He always strove to be 'his best' and not necessarily 'the best'. He helped establish over 30 AIDS care centers in Asia, providing life-saving medical services to over 30,000 people living with AIDS. He was awarded the prestigious Royal Order of Sahametri by the Royal government of Cambodia in 2008. He is preoccupied with making HIV treatment more effective with the use of newer drugs and therapy and the challenge of managing the side-effects of these drugs. He feels it is crucial to continue and constantly educate doctors, nurses and other HIV healthcare providers. He has worked in collaboration with various Ministries of Health in India, China, Cambodia, Thailand, Nepal and Vietnam.

Three years ago, Chinkholal gave up his chair at the American Healthcare Organization to take a break. "I need to follow my heart," he says with conviction. Having seen enough of social and professional discrimination to the point that some care providers did not even touch their AIDS patients, he decided to bring about a more humane approach to patients with HIV. "I have seen the power of a concerned caring touch and its impact on patients. It made me think of the human touch, as an essential and integral part of healing and therefore giving hope," he says. This was what led him to nurture the foundation, his current pet project, the Touch of Hope Foundation (THF) that he set up in 1993. One of the salient features of THF is to be human and compassionate to those who are suffering. Chinkholal is determined to change lives and be a paragon of change himself. In less than two years of working on his foundation, THF has provided humane, holistic services to over 1,000 HIV patients and reached out to over 3,000 family members of people living with the virus. The Abundant Life Project supports AIDS-infected and vulnerable children's education. The income generation project especially for widows has revived hope and brought smiles to many faces. His work has just begun and he is keen to spread his compassionate care model in India and beyond. Would life be any different or better if he was a footballer or a bureaucrat of sorts? Chinkholal has no regrets whatsoever; he's always

frank cheerful and devoid of airs, as he redefines the exist-
ing methods of health care and keeps hope alive each day.
He has indeed gained a legendary status in the fight against
AIDS the world over.

BIOGRAPHER

Hoihnu Hauzel is an independent journalist
based in Gurgaon. She has been a journalist for
15 years, having worked for the *Asian Age, Indian
Express, Hindustan Times,* The *Times of India,* The
Telegraph. She authored the first-ever compre-
hensive cookbook on Northeastern recipes.She
is a recipient of Thomson Reuters Fellowship for
writing International News, London. She continues to write on travel, hospitality, art and lifestyle
for different publications in India.

*How can I be useful? Of what service can I be? The day I
understood the answers to these questions was the day I
unleashed my true potential.*

– Jeroninio

Acknowledgments

The inspiration for the *Karma Kurry* series of books – and to share knowledge and encourage people to rise above the ordinary and become extraordinary by telling stories of unsung everyday heroes – comes from my father Wilfred Simon Almeida who left this world when I was eight. Every time someone remembers him, they fondly speak about how he loved reading and also encouraged them to read and become something more.

This book has taken almost two years to fructify and it has been possible only because of Meenu Chopra, Hunar Brar and Jyoti Nanda who helped with the compilation and editing of all the stories. Our second book in the series is also ready and shall be launched soon after the release of the first book.

I wish I also wish to thank Bosco Fernandes for having initiated our collaboration with Jaico to thank all the people whose stories are featured in this book for their whole-hearted support and their chosen biographers who brought these stories to life. I also take this opportunity to thank Anurag Nirbhaya and Sukhbir Singh who are big pillars of support for the iCONGO institution and all we do. My sincere thanks to Amit Shahi and Sudhir Horo from The Idea Works, Rashmi Ranjan from Cranberry Communications and Josy Paul, Ajai Jhala and Sandipan Bhattacharyya from BBDO for all the creative support they have contributed for all our campaigns and movements.

I extend my sincere thanks to Sridhar Reddy, CMD of CtrlS, and an old friend, philanthropist and supporter, who has helped us to sustain the Karmaveer movement. His noble story should have been featured in this book but he has been too modest. My sincere thanks to Karan Paul, Chairman and Renu Kakkar, Director CSR & Corporate Communications of the Apeejay Surrendra Group, who have partnered us in our mission to Democratize Heroism through Karma Yuga – RIGHT every WRONG generation. For the past few years, I have been developing and enhancing my skills as a Teacher, Leadership Trainer and Coach for working with people to fulfill their fundamental duties and practice human values. For this I would like to thank Rajan Kaicker, Lavleen Raheja and Gaurav Raheja, Directors of Franklin Covey South Asia who have made a huge contribution in my advanced learning, supported me to hone my skills and encouraged me to keep on learning.

I also wish to express my sincere thanks to everyone at Jaico Publishing House for their support and solidarity. They have been most proactive about this book and have promised to leave no stone unturned to take these stories to one and all for inspiring them to be the change. My special thanks to the people at Jaico Publishing House who are closely involved with this project: Ashwin Shah, Akash Shah, Rayasam Sharma, Sandhya Iyer, Savita Rao, Disha Jayadeep, Vijay Thakur and all others.

My younger sisters Effie and Lisa; and younger brothers Archie and Vivian have always inspired me to be more, learn more and become more. I take this opportunity to express my love for them.

I also wish to thank my paternal Uncle Wilson Almeida and step father Bevin Martins for all their mentoring and guidance in my growing up years.

My sons Zorawar and Ransher and niece Emily, who are the future along with all the children of the world, have inspired me to do whatever little I can do in my sphere of influence to create a legacy of a better planet for future generations. The stories in the book are for people of all generations to know that each of us needs to do our little bit to serve humanity, as service is the rent we pay to occupy our space on earth. When we do something to be the change in our world, it is not purely altruistic because if we help create a better world, it will also benefit our children. Yes, we are in the same boat and we need to remember the native American wisdom that we do not inherit the earth from our ancestors, but borrow it from our children. Hence, it is imperative that each of us does our part to create a better, safer world where our future generations, our children can eat, breathe, sleep, play and live in a safe environment and society.

The best for the last, I wish to thank the two women who are pillars of strength in my life – my mother Betty Lucia Torquato Martins who worked hard to provide me with every opportunity to excel after my father's death. Thank you, Mum, for everything and for always being there. Love you. And my wife Jugnu Grewal Almeida who encourages me to have my head in the clouds, push the limit and be relentless, while ensuring that I always have my feet on the ground and never lose touch with reality. I love you J and thank you so much for all the wonderful gifts you brought in my life, including Mama and Dad (Mini Grewal and Col. Randhir Singh Grewal) and my most precious gifts, our sons.

About the Authors

Jeroninio Almeida (affectionately called Jerry, the Karma teacher by friends and associates) is an internationally certified life coach, leadership trainer, management consultant and teacher, and also serves as an empanelled subject matter expert with the world's biggest training and coaching mission headquartered in the US. Jerry works as a coach with three veteran ministers, some young parliamentarians, several CEOs/CXOs and leadership teams in companies to help them achieve their optimum potential in their personal and professional lives. Jerry is a certified master practitioner of Neuro-linguistic programming (NLP), EnneaGram of personality, Gestalt therapy and Logo therapy. He is a keen observer and eternal learner of Eastern Wisdom like Reiki, Kaizen, Hypnotherapy, human & organisation behavior, social sciences, ancient sciences and literature.

His clients include several Fortune 100 and 500 companies, Navratna Public Sector Enterprises (PSEs), small and medium enterprises (SMES), UN organizations, international NGOs, B-schools, colleges, schools and grassroots community organizations. Jerry is a highly sought after professional motivational speaker and a celebrated inspirational orator. He speaks in numerous annual meetings of top companies and global forums organized by the UN, World Economic Forum, World Social Forum, World Affairs Council, US Embassy, Commonwealth Youth Program, British Council, Rotary International, YEO, **Confederation of**

Indian Industry (CII) and the list is endless. He also serves as visiting faculty at several B-schools like the **Indian School of Business** (ISB), **IPER, SOIL, Management Development Institute** (MDI) and Xavier Institute of Management (XIM) and has spoken in forums organized by INSEAD and Harvard University

Jerry, who has been a serial entrepreneur in media, advertising, dotcom and entertainment ventures in his earlier life, is now a missionary entrepreneur (he does not like social entrepreneur since he feels most of the people in the social venture sector are also chasing profits and not CHANGE and thus coined the term **Noble Missionary Entrepreneurs for people with a primary and core objective of doing good for society**) and a firebrand human, animal & environmental rights activist. He has effectively and successfully founded/created movements like '**The Joy of Giving**' which has shaped into a huge national crusade and is being emulated in other countries. He has started other movements like '**Karma Yuga – the Right Every Wrong Generation**' and '**REX – Ideas for Action CONCLiVE**'. He also founded iCONGO, the International Confederation of NGOs and has been instrumental in creating the **KarmaVeer Puraskaar, global awards for social justice and citizen action which were termed by Dr. Varghese Kurian as the most ethical and credible awards.** Jerry also founded the **KarmaVeer Chakra Awards** in partnership with the UN to celebrate extraordinary heroes who are making a difference in our world everyday. His simple mantra, is that **I Change to change India and the World** and if you are performing those simple actions to be the change and make a difference , than you can earn the **KarmaVeer Chakra award** and maybe even be featured in future **Karma Kurry** books.

Jerry, who is driven to make a difference in the world, has come up with brilliant alternative ideas to create awareness and has produced his first Bollywood movie *Ek Alag Mausam* to promote dignity for people living with HIV. He has also created a venture fund 'iCOZFLIX' (a Public Advocacy Cinema Fund), which produced the national award-winning Hindi film *I AM*. It was the first Indian movie to have been made with funds raised through crowd sourcing. In 2009, he partnered with the The Ramon Magsaysay award winner Neelima Mishra to create a caring capital to empower poor farmers become self-sustained. The caring capital model and his other work for society earned Jerry The Ramon Magsaysay award nomination which he humbly declined, as he follows a strict 'no award' policy. He feels that there is a lot more to do before resting on laurels and accolades. Jerry has also received nominations for the Eisenhower Fellowships, the Yale World Fellows Program and the Young Global Leaders award by the World Economic Forum.

Jerry believes that every person can be a hero, a leader and a teacher who can help create more leaders, heroes and teachers. Jerry's mission in life is to help people awaken that hero, leader and teacher within, as he believes that when we do our part to right a wrong, only then together as *One,* we can *right* every *wrong* and collectively change the world. Jerry has now dedicated his life to train teachers with transformational leadership skills which can be imparted to children and youth. He has created a powerful concept as a teacher to instill pride and power in all teachers; **not just teachers, but awakeners, enlighteners and transformers.** He has created the simple but powerful idea of 'we as teachers can see, touch and change the future' by working with children, to help them become everyday heroes.

Jerry lives in Gurgaon with his wife Jugnu Grewal Almeida and sons, Zorawar and Ransher.

For more information about Jerry and his work, visit www.jerrylearns2learn.com

Jyoti Nanda

Jyoti has been connected with the education industry for the last three decades. She has taught in both mainstream schools as well as schools for the differently abled. Besides a Masters' degree in history and a B.Ed, Jyoti also has a diploma in educational management. She has also done a basic course in audio and speech therapy.

The aspiration to learn and acquire new skills motivated her to move to the publishing industry. Her experience spans both the school and higher education publishing divisions. After a decade in the publishing industry, she moved to a learning and development consultancy as Head, Research. Her stint there helped her align her innermost beliefs and thoughts. A trained and certified life coach, she is interested in the concepts of life skills, motivation and leadership. Jyoti is also a Landmark Education Graduate and has attended the Dale Carnegie Train the Trainer Certificate Program.

Jyoti has published six textbooks on environmental studies for pre-primary and primary classes.

Currently, she is working as General Manager, QA and Training with Macmillan; and she also conducts workshops for school teachers and principals.

JAICO PUBLISHING HOUSE
Elevate Your Life. Transform Your World.

ESTABLISHED IN 1946, Jaico Publishing House is home to world-transforming authors such as Sri Sri Paramahansa Yogananda, Osho, The Dalai Lama, Sri Sri Ravi Shankar, Robin Sharma, Deepak Chopra, Jack Canfield, Eknath Easwaran, Devdutt Pattanaik, Khushwant Singh, John Maxwell, Brian Tracy and Stephen Hawking.

Our late founder Mr. Jaman Shah first established Jaico as a book distribution company. Sensing that independence was around the corner, he aptly named his company Jaico ('Jai' means victory in Hindi). In order to service the significant demand for affordable books in a developing nation, Mr. Shah initiated Jaico's own publications. Jaico was India's first publisher of paperback books in the English language.

While self-help, religion and philosophy, mind/body/spirit, and business titles form the cornerstone of our non-fiction list, we publish an exciting range of travel, current affairs, biography, and popular science books as well. Our renewed focus on popular fiction is evident in our new titles by a host of fresh young talent from India and abroad. Jaico's recently established Translations Division translates selected English content into nine regional languages.

Jaico's Higher Education Division (HED) is recognized for its student-friendly textbooks in Business Management and Engineering which are in use countrywide.

In addition to being a publisher and distributor of its own titles, Jaico is a major national distributor of books of leading international and Indian publishers. With its headquarters in Mumbai, Jaico has branches and sales offices in Ahmedabad, Bangalore, Bhopal, Bhubaneswar, Chennai, Delhi, Hyderabad, Kolkata and Lucknow.

SINCE 1946